HOW TO FRANCHISE YOUR BUSINESS

The plain speaking guide for business owners

CLIVE SAWYER

lıp

First published in 2011 by:

Live It Publishing
27 Old Gloucester Road
London, United Kingdom.
WC1N 3AX
www.liveitpublishing.com

This book is designed to provide accurate and authoritative general information in regard to the subject matter covered. As each business is unique in its requirements, this book is sold with the understanding that neither the author nor publisher are giving specific business, financial or legal advice. The services of a competent professional should be sought prior to the implementation of any expansion models for your business.

Photographs courtesy of Steve Bishop Photography
www.stevebishopphotography.com

ISBN 978-1-906954-19-2 (pbk)

Dedicated to

Suzy, Henry & Lizzie

CONTENTS

Section 5 - Useful Information 256

FOREWORD

Clive Sawyer has designed this book to give the reader an insight into how to successfully franchise a business. Using plain speaking Clive has delivered an insightful and thorough overview which will become essential reading for business owners considering franchising their business as an option for growth.

Ensuring business owners embarking on the franchising route are better informed is clearly a worthy objective and one that is delivered in the chapters of this publication. What I particularly like about this book is the intention to provide a plain speaking guide which will prove to be a useful reference point for people at any stage of their franchising journey.

Franchising has many potential benefits for businesses. It is vital that anyone considering franchising seeks the guidance and support of an experienced and reputable British Franchise Association accredited consultant such as Clive. Far too many business owners take their first steps towards franchising without seeking the professional advice that they clearly need and consequently set themselves up for a big fall.

This book is a serious attempt to make sure business owners understand the processes required to correctly franchise their business and to ensure that they can make a considered decision about their franchising options. If after reading this book you decide franchising is not the right option for your business, do not despair! Clive will have provided you an equally valuable service as he will have done for those who are reassured that franchising their business is the best expansion option for them.

Richard Holden
Head of Franchising
Lloyds Banking Group
<u>www.lloydstsb.com/franchising</u>

INTRODUCTION

I have been involved in franchising for many years advising and helping companies of all sizes to successfully franchise both in the UK and internationally. There are many books written on the subject of how to franchise a business, however in my opinion the majority appear to be written with the intention of making the topic seem more complicated than it actually is.

In reality, the steps required to successfully franchise are the same skills that are necessary in the running of any successful business. It is my belief that my role as a professional franchise adviser should be to supplement those existing business skills with advice and guidance on those areas that are very specific to franchising.

Franchising done properly can be an excellent way for a business to expand, regionally, nationally and/or internationally. However, franchising is not right for every business. It is therefore important before setting out on the franchising route to first understand what franchising is and then what is involved in setting up and running a successful franchise business.

My objective in writing this book is to provide an accessible tool that clearly outlines the steps that are required to franchise a business. This book will explain, in a logical, uncomplicated and plain speaking manner, everything a business owner will need to know in order to help them decide whether franchising is right for them and their business. If the decision is to franchise, the business owner will know what the various steps are and which areas they will need to supplement their own business acumen, using the assistance of a specialist franchise adviser.

If you decide franchising is the right way to grow your business, I wish you every good fortune and hope that this book will be the first step in successfully franchising your business. Should you decide having read this book, that perhaps franchising is not the right way forward then do not despair as there are a variety of other ways to expand and grow a business, which are to be dealt with in more detail in the last chapters of this book.

Clive Sawyer
Managing Director
Business Options
<u>www.businessoptions.biz</u>

SECTION 1

The Franchise Development Model

Section 1 will explain what is meant by franchising and how a business owner can assess whether franchising is right for them. It will take an-in depth look at the Franchise Development Model, the most crucial element of the whole franchising process.

If one gets the Franchise Development Model right it will make all the rest of the steps in franchising your business much easier. Due to the importance and scale of the Franchise Development Model, I have broken it down into three manageable parts.

This section has been split into four chapters:

Chapter 1 - Franchising a Business
This will explain what is meant by the term franchising and allows a business to assess whether franchising is the right way forward and if it is, how they will know whether now is the right time to do it.

Chapter 2 - The Franchise Development Model - Part 1
This will explain the reasons for creating a Franchise Development Model, list all the various sections that should be included within it and discuss the first of the sections in depth.

Chapter 3 - The Franchise Development Model - Part 2
Part two of the Franchise Development Model will look at the critical legal

considerations which make up the terms of the Franchise Agreement.

Chapter 4 - **The Franchise Development Model - Part 3**
Part three will look at the remaining elements of the Franchise Development Model. It will discuss the various roles and responsibilities for both the franchisor and the franchisee. It will then explain how to create a franchisee profile enabling the franchisor to identify the type of person most suited to become a successful franchisee for them. It will then cover the various obligations for both the franchisor and franchisee and finally the type of financial projections that need to be created.

Chapter 1

FRANCHISING A BUSINESS

What is Franchising?

When people talk about franchising what they are normally referring to is "Full Business Format Franchising".

The British Franchise Association (bfa) defines franchising as:

> "... the granting of a licence by one person (the franchisor) to another (the franchisee), which entitles the franchisee to trade under the trade mark/trade name of the franchisor and to make use of an entire package, comprising all the elements necessary to establish a previously untrained person in the business and to run it with continual assistance on a predetermined basis."
>
> **The British Franchise Association (bfa)**

The International Franchise Association (IFA) defines franchising as:

" ... A franchise is the agreement or license between two legally independent parties which gives a person or group of people (franchisee) the right to market a product or service using the trademark or trade name of another business (franchisor). The franchisee has the right to market a product or service using the operating methods of the franchisor. The franchisee has an obligation to pay the franchisor fees for these rights whilst the franchisor has the obligation to provide rights and support to franchisees."

The International Franchise Association (IFA)

In simple terms, the franchisor grants a franchisee the right to operate a business using the franchised company's name, branding, products and or services, systems and processes that the franchisor has successfully and profitably operated themselves.

Before going any further it is worth ensuring that it is clear "who is who" in the franchise relationship. The franchisor is the company that is franchising their business. The franchisee is the person who buys the franchise from the franchisor.

In addition to granting of rights to the franchisee, the franchisor also needs to:

- continually develop the products and services that the franchisee sells, ensuring that they remain current and competitive in the marketplace.

- provide ongoing support and guidance to the franchisee.

In return, the franchisee usually pays an initial upfront fee and then ongoing monthly fees for the duration that they have the franchise.

When one thinks of Full Business Format Franchising, the best example is probably McDonalds; McDonalds is the epitome of Full Business Format franchising. Wherever you go in the world you can be confident about what a Big Mac will taste like, how you will be served and the total McDonalds experience.

McDonalds is the epitome of Full Business Format franchising

Are you ready to franchise?

The fact that you are reading this indicates that you either believe that franchising is the right way to expand your business, or you wish to find out more about what is involved in franchising a business. Franchising may be the right way to expand your business however there are a number of elements that need to be in place before you can start franchising.

Do you have a profitable trading track record?

The whole concept of franchising is based on the premise that if a franchisee follows the franchisor's business system exactly the franchisee should be able to make similar profits. Therefore, your business must have profitable trading history over a period of time.

The exact length of profitable trading history before one should franchise is debatable. Clearly, the longer a business has traded profitable the better. A company that has been trading profitably for ten years is obviously in a much better position to franchise than a company that has only traded for two years. I am often asked, what is the minimum length of time that a business should have traded before they start to franchise? This is a difficult question to answer but if I was to stick my neck out I would say eighteen months. I am sure that many people within the franchise community will be throwing their arms up at my suggestion of such a short trading history. The reason I say eighteen months is made with the knowledge that it takes a minimum six months to get from the position of deciding to franchise to being ready to market the franchise opportunity. During this time the business will continue to trade and therefore will have two years trading behind them by the time they start offering franchises.

Two years is still a short trading history on which to model a franchise, however there has to be a degree of commercial pragmatism. If you operate in a sector that is proven and your trading history mirrors your competitors when they started, then I believe that it should be possible to have a degree of confidence regarding your future trading history. Confidence on its own is not sufficient; I believe that businesses franchising with only two years of trading history have a responsibility to make it clear to prospective franchisees of the greater risk compared with a company that has been trading longer.

There are a number of people that actively look for a franchise with a young company. They acknowledge that their risks may be higher however they will have the opportunity to get in at the beginning and may have more influence over the way the business develops compared with a well established business.

You cannot franchise a failing or unprofitable business

The underlining premise however does not change, the business needs to be profitable and be able to demonstrate a successful trading history. You cannot franchise a failing or unprofitable business otherwise all your franchisees will fail.

Do you need to run a pilot first?

Again I believe there is no definitive answer to this question. Clearly it is more advantageous if you have operated the business in more than one location as it provides additional proof that the business can be successful in other parts of the country.

When franchising, most businesses are looking to take on franchisees in different parts of the country. Therefore it is important that you know that your business can be successful throughout the country. Just because your product or service is wanted where you are located doesn't necessarily mean that it will be equally popular in other parts of the country. Something that is popular in the South of England will not necessarily be popular in the Midlands or the North. Therefore before franchising you need to be confident that franchisees throughout the country can achieve the level of business that you are projecting. The best way of doing this is by setting up outlets in different parts of the country yourself. However, the reason why many people choose to franchise their business is because they don't want to or can't afford to open additional outlets. So how can you be sure that your business can succeed in other parts of the country?

Although not a complete replacement for first hand experience, I believe that certain businesses can look to their competitors for the proof. If for instance you operate a take away burger business in London then I believe that you do not have to operate an outlet in Birmingham to know that people in Birmingham will buy your burgers. Additionally there may be regional factors that need to be considered such the price you can charge and the number of competitors in each area, however if these are taken into account then I believe that a business can legitimately franchise having only operated in one place with one outlet.

One of the biggest reasons franchises fail is lack of funds

Do you have the funds to franchise?

One of the biggest reasons franchises fail or franchisors struggle to recruit franchisees is due to lack of funds. In the UK there are no specific franchise laws. This means that there is nothing stopping a company franchising their business themselves without external specialist franchise help. Even when it comes to the Franchise Agreement and other legal documents, a business can theoretically write these themselves. The trouble with doing everything oneself with no expert advice is that you are likely to make mistakes. You may not know the mistakes that other businesses have made in the past when franchising and the actions needed to prevent similar mistakes happening to your business. Additionally, if you create your own legal documents it may mean that if you were to take legal action to protect your franchise and the investment of your franchise network, it is unlikely to stand up in court. Buying template franchise documents off the internet is also unlikely to give the protection you and your franchisees need, since the documents cannot address all the specific factors relevant to your business as by their nature template documents are very general.

Often when a business assesses the cost to franchise their business they overlook the costs of any developments required to their existing infrastructure. Many businesses do not already have the systems and processes in place to support a nationwide network. This is not entirely surprising as many businesses will only be operating in a local area and will have had no need to put such systems and processes in place to manage people across the country. However, updating or replacing existing systems and processes can be expensive and businesses need to budget for this when assessing their funding requirement.

As a very general guide, I advise businesses considering franchising that they will need in the region of £25,000 to get them to a position where they are ready to start marketing their franchise opportunity. This however excludes the cost of any development to their internal systems and processes or the cost of piloting their business if they need to do pilot.

In addition to the cost of getting a business to a position where it is ready to start marketing a franchise opportunity, the business must also allow for a specific budget for the cost of marketing the franchise. I see a lot of businesses that spend all their money developing their franchise and do not have sufficient money to market their franchise. In Section Three – Franchise Recruitment, I discuss the various ways to effectively market a franchise, however at this stage in relation to funding requirements, a business should budget about £2,000 per month for the cost of marketing their franchise. Given that franchisors, even when they receive interest on the first day of marketing their franchise opportunity, are unlikely to sign up a franchisee and receive their first franchise licence fee for at least six to eight weeks, it is important to budget for at least six months of marketing expenditure when working out your initial funding requirement.

When one starts to add the cost to franchise it is easy to see that you will need in excess of £40,000 and it could be considerably more if you need to put in new systems and processes or need to set up a pilot operation. However, when put in the perspective of starting to develop a national brand through company outlets, it's inexpensive.

Do you have the time to spend on franchising your business?

It is important to be fully informed of the impact franchising your business will have on your time. Do you have the time and commitment to give ongoing support to your franchisees? When I say ongoing support, I do not mean giving franchisees a phone call once a month to see how they are doing. Ongoing support is about taking a real interest in the success of your franchisees and helping them to be as successful as possible. The worse thing you can have in a franchise network is failing franchisees. Failing franchisees will not only take much more of your time, but they will affect the level of ongoing fee income you receive, whilst also making future

Nobody wants to buy a franchise that has unhappy failing franchisees

franchisee recruitment much harder. Nobody wants to buy a franchise that has unhappy failing franchisees.

In addition, having sufficient time to allocate to developing a franchise is often under estimated. When a company employs the services of experienced franchise consultants and franchise lawyers, there will still be considerable time implications for the company.

A word of warning, do not be misled by claims from franchise consultancies that advertise that they will do everything for you; even if they could, which in reality hardly ever happens, is this what is best for your business? If your franchise is going to be structured around the specifics of your business and you are going to support your franchisees to ensure they are successful, this cannot be done without your personal involvement. I believe the best franchises are ones where business owners take an active role in the development of their franchise and work alongside experienced franchise specialists. However the time involvement needs to be factored in at the outset. You need to ask yourself whether you can spare the time from your core work and will the business suffer whilst you are spending time on the franchise development? It may be that you need to take on additional resources to cover some of your work whilst you are concentrating on your franchise development. If this is the case, the cost of this additional resource needs to be factored in to the overall funding requirement.

Do you want to be liable for the products and services sold?

Liability is normally a major concern when businesses look to expand. Businesses often worry about how they will be able to control the way their products or services are sold nationwide. What happens if a salesperson makes false claims or miss sells? Does this mean that the company is liable for their actions? One of the benefits with franchising is that the franchisee is liable for their own actions, not you as the franchisor. The legal contract for the sale of any product or service is between the customer and the franchisee. The only time that you, as the franchisor, could be liable is when a franchisee has been told by you how to sell a product or service and the information you provided contravened laws, or if you provided the franchisee with the products they sell and the products were faulty. However, having said this, it doesn't matter what expansion model you adopt, if your products are faulty or you tell people how to sell them incorrectly, you will always be liable.

One of the benefits of franchising is that the franchisee is liable for their own actions

Do you want your franchisees to trade under your brand name?

It is important to understand that if franchisees are going to trade under your brand name then systems and processes will need to be put in place to protect the reputation of your brand from any poor performing franchisees in your network.

Do you believe you are ready to franchise?

Hopefully assessing your readiness to franchise has not put you off the idea of franchising; however, it really is essential that you are fully aware of the implications of franchising your business BEFORE you start. If you believe that your business is suitable for franchising and you have the resources both in time and financially, what next?

The next step is no different from any business project that a company wants to implement. With any project, however big or small, it is essential to develop a plan. The plan will work out the key components of the project which will be the basis for all the implementation phases of the project. In franchising, this planning phase is either called the Franchise Feasibility Study or as I prefer to refer to it, the Franchise Development Model. The next chapters will look at the Franchise Development Model, explaining who it is for, what it should contain, and how it should be used.

Chapter 2

THE FRANCHISE DEVELOPMENT MODEL - PART 1

The Franchise Development Model is the most crucial step in your whole franchise development. This is because without having a clear plan of how your franchise needs to be structured to make it successful for both you as the franchisor and your future franchisees, there is virtually no chance that you will get it right.

If you get the planning right at this stage everything else will follow as you will have a blueprint for all the other steps required in franchising. You will know what needs to be included within all the franchise legal documentation and what needs to be included within the Franchise Operations Manual. The roles and responsibilities for both franchisor and franchisee will be clear as will be the criteria for creating Franchise Territories. The cost of the franchise and the profitability for both franchisor and franchisee will have been identified. There will be a clear method for developing the Franchise Recruitment Strategy based on the franchisee profile that has been created. Finally it will be clear what needs to be included within the Franchisee Recruitment Material as the Franchise

> *The most important element of any franchise is the Franchise Development Model*

Development Model will have identified the type of person being targeted as a franchisee, the franchise offering and the way franchisees will operate.

The Franchise Development Model also allows you to structure the internal resources that you may require to support your franchisees, help you develop the franchisee training programme and help people interested in becoming a franchisee of yours to develop a business plan and to approach funding sources. In short the most important element of any franchise is the Franchise Development Model.

What should be included with a Franchise Development Model?

Without wishing to over simplify the question, it should include everything. However there are a number of core elements that any Franchise Development Model should include, these being:

- The Franchise Package
- The Terms of the Franchise
- The Role of the Franchisee and the Franchisor
- The Franchisee Profile
- The Financial Projections for both the Franchisee and Franchisor
- The Obligations for both the Franchisee and Franchisor

The Franchise Package

The Franchise Package includes the Initial Franchise Fee, the Franchise Set-Up Package, the Franchisee Working Capital requirement, any additional capital costs for the franchisee, the total investment required for the franchise, and the payment terms.

The Initial Franchise Fee

This is the fee paid to become a franchisee. It normally includes the cost of training the franchisee and loan of the Franchise Operations Manual. The Initial Franchisee Fee is usually relatively low and in the region of £5,000 to £20,000. When people see a franchise advertised for £200,000 it is important to understand that this isn't just the Initial Franchise Fee but that it will also include the Franchise Set-Up Package and most likely the Working Capital that franchisees will require. Although there are no laws or regulations that restrict the level of the Initial Franchise Fee, the British Franchise Association (bfa) and most professionals within the Franchise Industry do not look favourably as a rule on Initial Franchise Fees which are in excess of £15,000. This is because the whole concept of franchising should be structured so that the franchisor has a vested interest in the success of their franchisees and the financial return for the franchisor is intrinsically linked to the franchisees' success.

Where a franchise is structured in such a way that the franchisor could make large amounts from selling franchises, there is a real temptation that the franchisor sells to anyone with access to the necessary funds, regardless as to their suitability as a franchises. There are instances of franchisors charging high Initial Franchise Fees who are prepared to sell their franchise to anyone, and as a result they have large numbers of franchisees that fail. The franchisor then takes back the franchise, with no recompense to the franchisee, and resells the franchise. In these cases the franchise is purely an upfront sales business for the franchisor.

The Franchise Operations Manual is only loaned to the franchisee

As previously mentioned the Initial Franchise Fee includes loan of the Franchise Operations Manual. The Franchise

Operations Manual is only loaned to the franchisee rather than being given to the franchisee, as it is contains highly confidential information about the running of the franchised business that the franchisor would not want to end up in the hands of its competitors. If the Franchise Operations Manual was given to the franchisee, then the franchise would be at liberty to do what they like with it.

The Franchise Set-Up Package

Most franchises are sold as turnkey businesses. This means the franchisee buys the franchise and the franchisor provides them with everything they need to operate their business. This has distinct advantages to both franchisor and the franchisee.

From the franchisor's perspective, it ensures that the set-up of each franchise can be done identically. The franchisor can source all the necessary equipment from suppliers that they have approved. Where the franchise is operated out of retail premises, the franchisor can ensure that the shop fitters used are approved and will ensure that the end result is exactly in line with the franchisor's requirements.

From the franchisee's perspective, a turnkey franchise is very attractive as there is much less time and involvement on their part in the setting up of their franchise. It also likely that many franchisees have never had to set up a business before and therefore even with detailed guidance, could make mistakes.

The content of the Franchise Set-Up Package will vary with each franchise. For a restaurant the Franchise Set-Up Package would include the equipping of the kitchens and front of house. It would include all the tables, chairs, crockery, glasses, tills, menus etc. In short everything the business needs to operate. With a pet food delivery franchise the Franchise Set-Up package may include a van, initial stock, marketing brochures, a sat nav etc. The Set-Up Package should include everything the franchisee needs to operate their pet food delivery franchise.

One key element that I believe should be included in all Franchise Set-Up Packages is an initial launch Marketing Campaign. When any franchisee starts, it is important both from a financial and motivational perspective that they have success early on. The best way to ensure this is to run a launch marketing campaign to let potential customers know about the franchisees business.

An initial launch Marketing Campaign should be included in all Franchise Set-Up Packages

There are two trains of thought when it comes to who should manage the launch marketing campaign, the franchisor or the franchisee. In most cases I believe that the franchisor is best placed to ensure it actually happens. If the launch Marketing Campaign is included in the Franchise Set-Up Package, it ensures that the franchisor has the money to implement the launch Marketing Campaign in its entirety. There are many cases where responsibility for the launch Marketing Campaign is passed to the franchisee and either only partial happens or doesn't happen at all.

A common and easy mistake for franchisees is to hold back on implementing any launch Marketing Campaign. Often this is due to a misplaced belief that they should generate business and income first to fund it. Clearly this is a mistake as without a tailored launch Marketing Campaign, customers will not know about the franchisees business. If a franchisor takes control of the initial launch Marketing Campaign, it ensures that it will happen properly, which gives the franchisee the best chance for early success, motivating them and providing a firm foundation to grow upon. If the franchisor's income is linked to the income of the franchisee, early success will generate greater income for the franchisor as well.

Working Capital

It is important that all franchisees have sufficient working capital to let them operate effectively, especially in the early months of their business whilst they are establishing themselves. Once the franchisee is up and running it is important that they have sufficient working capital to run their business without having to wait on income generated from customers to fund their activities. This may include paying staff and suppliers on time, or undertaking marketing activities. For this reason, it is usual to stipulate a minimum level of working capital that franchisees will need to start their business and also the minimum amount of working capital received during their franchise.

Additional Costs

Although many franchises are sold as turnkey businesses, there are still items of expenditure that the franchisee may have which are down to them to fund directly. These costs could include items such as the franchisees legal costs in purchasing the franchise, any premium the franchisee needs to pay, on a particular commercial premises, they want to operate from, the requirement to have a vehicle for use within the business where a vehicle isn't included within the Set-Up package. If the franchise is to be run from home the related costs of adapting/fitting out a room in the franchisees home where the franchise will be run from also need to be taken into account. It is important that the prospective franchisee is aware of all additional costs that they may incur to ensure that they have sufficient funds to meet them without compromising the operation of their business.

The Total Investment

Most franchisees are only concerned with how much the franchise will cost in total, to allow them to arrange the necessary funds. The individual costs of the Initial Franchise Fee, the Set-Up Package, the Working Capital and any additional costs they may have are less important than the Total Investment.

Sometimes franchisors try not to highlight all the costs involved as they want to appear cheaper than other competing franchises and believe that by under pricing the competition it will make them more likely to recruit franchisees. It may be that they do attract more interest in their franchise however; the franchisee will still need the full amount of funding if they are going to stand a chance of being successful. If they are not informed of the total investment required it may be that they struggle in their business through under funding. If the franchisor only reveals the true level of investment required later in the recruitment process, the prospective franchisee may either not be able to raise the additional funds and will have to pull out wasting both the franchisor's and the prospective franchisee's time, or the prospective franchisees finds the additional funding

Prospective franchisees must know from the start what their total investment is going to be

but lose trust in the franchisor. A loss of trust between prospective franchisee and franchisor at the outset is a recipe for future problems. Therefore make sure that your prospective franchisees know what their total investment is going to be from the start.

Payment Terms

The final element of the Franchise Package is to decide on the payment terms. When it comes to the Initial Franchise Fee it is usual for franchisors, having interviewed and identified a suitable candidate to be a franchisee, to require a deposit before release of the Franchise Agreement. This deposit shows commitment from the prospective franchisee ensuring large amounts of time are not wasted on individuals that are not really committed to become a franchisee. In return for paying a deposit it is usual for a franchisor to take no further enquiries for the particular territory, whilst the prospective franchisee reviews the Franchise Agreement. The franchisor will usually stipulate a timescale in which the prospective franchisee must make a decision, such as thirty days from receipt of the Franchise Agreement. Should a prospective franchisee decide having reviewed the Franchise Agreement or for any other reason, that they are no longer interested in the franchise it is usual for the franchisor to return the deposit less any direct costs the franchisor has incurred. The British Franchise Association's rules state:

> *"Pre-contract deposits must be refunded to prospective franchisees that (regardless of reason) withdraw their application, less any direct costs, and as actually incurred. Costs that, if related to the particular candidate can legitimately be deducted from any refund include, but are not necessarily limited to: Solicitors, Accountants,*

Travel Costs, Food and accommodation, Paid research for the particular territory. Costs that cannot be legitimately deducted include but are not limited to: Opportunity costs e.g. the cost of a lost sale, staff costs."

The British Franchise Association (bfa)

It is usual for the balance of the Initial Franchisee Fee to be paid at the time the Franchise Agreement is signed.

Different franchisors choose different payment model approaches when it comes to the Franchisee Set-Up Package. Some franchisors ask for it to be paid in full at the time of signing the Franchise Agreement. Others ask for it to be paid a set time before the start of the franchisees training, and some ask for part of the Set-Up Package to be paid at the time the Franchise Agreement is signed with the balance due a set time before the franchisees training. The decision is usually based on how long after signing the Franchise Agreement the franchisee training will commence, as some franchisors only run franchisee training courses at specific times of the year. For franchises that require premises, there can also be a long delay whilst suitable premises are found and leases arranged. Where this occurs I believe it is a bit unreasonable for the franchisee to have to pay the Franchise Set-Up Package in full when they sign their Franchise Agreement only to have the franchisor sit on the funds for a long period of time.

Where payment terms are staggered it is important to ensure that the franchisee has all the funds available to them and that they are not utilising the gaps between payments to source additional funding.

In recent times, given the economic climate and difficulty prospective franchisees may experience in raising finance, I believe that it may be advantageous for franchisors to stagger the franchisees payment, therefore easing the burden on the franchisee in raising the full funding in one go. However I believe franchisors should only do so in the right circumstances. I do not see any reason why franchisors should not offer staggered payment terms instead of losing suitable prospective franchisees, since the franchisor will make the majority of their money from the ongoing success of their franchisees. I use the word suitable, because franchisors must be wary about offering prospective franchisees staggered payments if a franchisee is likely to struggle with having sufficient funds to operate their franchise properly. For the right franchisee and in the right circumstances I believe offering staggered payments rather than losing them makes sound business sense.

For the right franchisee offering staggered payments rather than losing them makes sound business sense

If you do offer staggered payments it is important to take legal advice as there are certain limits regulating the number of staged payments one can take before falling under commercial lending legislation.

Chapter 3

THE FRANCHISE DEVELOPMENT MODEL - PART 2

The second part of the Franchise Development Model is concerned with the terms under which the franchise will be operated.

The Terms of the Franchise

The terms of the franchise include amongst other things: details relating to the number of years the franchise will be granted for, the ongoing fee structure, the legal entity the franchisee must adopt, terms relating to VAT and Data Protection registration. It also includes the sale and renewal of the franchise, the premises that franchisees can operate from, the criteria for territories, the policy regarding national accounts, ongoing training of the franchisee and any staff they may have, and what happens if the franchisee is incapacitated or worse dies.

The Franchise Term

The majority of franchises are granted for 5 years. It is rare for franchises to be granted for less than 5 years although where the total investment is high, usually where retail premises are involved, longer franchise terms are offered to allow franchisees sufficient time to make a return on their investment.

There is no legislation that dictates the length of time a franchise should be granted for

There is no legislation that dictates the length of time a franchise should be granted for, so in the end it is down to each franchisor. The key issues that have an influence on the length of term are: the terms that competing franchises offer, how long it will take franchisees to make a reasonable return on their investment, and the perceived need for the franchisor to bring new blood into the network to keep the drive and commitment within the franchise network. If a franchise term is too long there is a risk that franchisees may become complacent after time losing motivation to grow their business further. Having the ability to bring new franchisees into the network can create new enthusiasm and help drive both individual franchises and the whole franchisee network forward.

Ongoing Fees

As previously discussed, franchisors make their money from charging franchisees a variety of fees throughout the duration of the franchise. The four key types of ongoing fees are:

1. Franchise Management Fee
2. National Marketing Fee
3. Mark-Up on Products supplied
4. Service Fees

1. The Franchise Management Fee, also referred to as a Royalty, is a charge made by the franchisor to cover their ongoing support to the franchisee and to generate a profit for the franchisor. There are usually two formats for the Franchise Management Fee, either a fixed monthly fee or a percentage of the franchisee's turnover. Where practical, my preference would be to link the Franchise Management Fee to a percentage of the franchisee's income. This ensures that the franchisor has a vested interest in helping the franchisee to be successful otherwise it can have a negative affect on the franchisors income stream. A number of franchisors prefer to charge a fixed monthly Franchise Management Fee. A fixed monthly Franchise Management Fee is easier to manage and the franchisor does not have to rely on the franchisee declaring their monthly income on which to base their fees on. The downside to a fixed Franchise Management Fee, especially from the franchisee's perspective, is that there is less incentive for a franchisor to help and support a franchisee as they

receive the same level of fee income regardless of the amount of support given.

Often franchisors that charge a fixed fee justify their decision to prospective franchisees by saying that the franchise doesn't have to pay an increase in fees when they increase their level of turnover. Often these franchisors may not be so "up front" and "vocal" when explaining that franchisees will still have to pay the same fixed fee even if their turnover reduces, and worse still even if their turnover is less than the fixed fee itself! I know of instances where franchisees on a fixed monthly fee did not generate sufficient income to even pay the fixed Franchise Management Fee let alone make any profit!

2. Charging a National Marketing Fee is a very normal practice in franchises. National Marketing Fees works on the principal that some marketing media are national and why should one franchisee pay to market themselves in national media that will benefit others franchisees in the network. Therefore a national marketing fee is charged whereby all franchisees pay a small amount each month and the franchisor uses these fees to undertake marketing for the benefit of the whole network. On television one will see a number of franchises that advertise their products or services such as McDonalds and Cash Generator. It would not be financially viable for any one franchise to have to pay for

television advertising and would also be unreasonable given that an advert on television will benefit all the franchisees in the network and not just the one paying for it. Therefore having all franchisees contributing a small amount to a national marketing fund that allows the franchisor to pay for such advertising makes sense and benefits the whole franchise network.

3. Where a franchisor sells products to the franchisee, it is usual that the franchisor will make a mark-up on the cost to the franchisee. The franchisor

Franchisee fees must be reasonable

should be able, due to the bulk buying ability or reduced in house manufacturing costs, mark-up the products they sell their franchisees and the products still be cheaper than the franchisees could purchase themselves. Problems can occur with product mark-ups where the franchisee is forced to purchase products from the franchisor although they could buy the exact same cheaper elsewhere. This leads to a feeling of bad will throughout the franchisee network and not surprisingly incidents of franchisees going behind the franchisors back and buying products elsewhere despite what is written in the Franchise Operations Manual and the Franchise Agreement.

4. Where a franchisor provides services to the franchisee, such as staff payroll, bookkeeping, customer invoice

issuing and collection, the franchisor will often charge separately for these services. The same issue relates to services provided to the franchisee as it does to mark-up on products. As long as the services provided by the franchisor can not be bought cheaper elsewhere, problems will not occur. Problems can occur however where the service charges are more expensive than if the franchisee used other service providers.

The overriding rule when it comes to franchisee fees is to make them reasonable and not to charge franchisees more for products or services that they can purchase from other sources.

Franchisee Legal Structure

As with any business, it is important to have the correct legal structure whether this is as a Sole Trader, Partnership or Limited Company. Many franchisors will stipulate the legal structure that franchisees must operate under however; others will leave it up to each individual franchisee.

Operating as a Sole Trader is the simplest way of starting a business with very few formalities. The individual will need to advise the Inland Revenue that they are self-employed for tax and National Insurance contributions.

Control of the business is entirely that of the Sole Trader and they are responsible for all management decisions. Sole Traders however, are personally responsible for any debts that they incur and, should the business fail, any personal assets that they have can be seized and sold to repay those debts. On the plus side, any profits that are made belong to the Sole Trader. Moreover, whilst a Sole Trader has a responsibility to maintain proper accounting records for tax and VAT purposes, any records that are kept are not available for public inspection.

In comparison a Limited Company is a separate legal entity from its members. The business is actually owned by the Limited Company, not by any one person. The major advantage with Limited Company's is that the liability of the company is as it sounds, limited. If the business fails, the personal assets of the members are usually protected. This is in contrast to the position where an individual operating as a Sole Trader has unlimited liability.

The ownership of a Limited Company is determined by the ownership of the shares in the company. The ownership of a company is separate from the management of the company. A company must have at least one director and one secretary. A Limited Company is governed by company law, mainly as contained in The Companies Act 1985. There are strict time limits, with penalties for failure, for filing documents, including company accounts, and members of the public can search the records and the accounts of any Limited Company. Directors are subject to regulations, and can be fined or even found guilty of a criminal offence for failure to comply.

From the franchisor's perspective there are often a number of considerations when deciding whether or not to stipulate a franchisee's corporate structure, such as having the ability to pursue the franchisee personally should they default on paying any fees. Another consideration would be whether the customers and suppliers of the franchisee would require them to be a certain legal entity to allow them to do business. The franchisor also needs to asses the effect the franchisees legal status may have on the franchisors brand as it may reflect better if the franchisees were all Limited Companies.

Many franchisors prefer to have their franchisees operate as Sole Traders. This means that the franchisee is likely for any debts they may accrue, whether they are to the franchisor, suppliers or customers. Despite franchisees operating as a totally independent business to the franchisor and any contracts they make whether they are between the franchisee and customer or the franchisee and suppliers, should a franchisee default, the customer or supplier may approach the franchisor for compensation. Although the franchisor will not have a legal responsibility to pay the debts of the franchisee, the franchisor may need to do so to protect the reputation of their brand. By having franchisees operating as Sole Traders makes it easier for the franchisor to take action against a franchisee compared with if they operated as a Limited Company.

In certain franchises, the franchisee's customer may have restrictions that mean they can only do business with Limited Companies. This is often the case where a franchisee is providing a service to large corporate customers, or where they are required to tender for contracts. In these cases it is important that the franchisee operates as a Limited Company.

With certain customers, dealing with a Limited Company rather than a Sole Trader gives a better impression. Clearly just because a company is a limited company, it does not necessarily mean that they are a better company than one that operates as a Sole Trader, however the customer's perception may be important to the franchisee in winning business.

Where the franchisor does not stipulate the legal entity for franchisees, the decision will come down to the personal circumstances of each individual franchisee. The Tax paid by Limited Company is often less than that paid by a Sole Trader. The tax advantages increase where net taxable profit is above the self employment upper earnings limit as money can be left in the business and therefore only subject to the Corporation Tax rate thereby avoiding the higher Sole Trader tax rate. However; a Limited Company requires it to have Directors and there are legal responsibilities and duties for Directors. Virtually in every circumstance, the advice to franchisees that are allowed to choose the legal status to operate their franchise under is to seek professional advice.

VAT Registration

As a franchisor the decision has to be taken as to whether franchisees are required to register for VAT before commencing their business or it is left up to the franchisee to decide, either when they feel the moment is right or when their turnover hits the VAT registration threshold.

> *Franchisees must get into the right mindset that they are running a business and not buying themselves a job!*

In many situations, if the projected turnover of the franchisee means that they are going to exceed the VAT registration threshold within their first year of trading; there is a strong argument to stipulate that franchisees must register for VAT from the outset. The saving to customers when a franchisee does not charge VAT is quickly negated by the problems faced when the franchisee has to increase their prices to include VAT. If a franchisee is going to have to register for VAT at some point, then for the business to be successful customers must be prepared to pay a VAT inclusive price. If the customer is not prepared to pay the price then the franchise is clearly going to fail.

I also believe that franchisees must get into the right mindset that they are running a business and not a buying themselves a job. Understanding that for most businesses VAT is something that goes with the territory will help them start their franchise with the right business mindset and help with future growth.

VAT registration also provides franchisors with an additional audit check on their franchisees. Where the franchisor's income is linked to the turnover of the franchisee, it is important that as many checks as possible are put in place to ensure that the turnover reported by the franchisee, on which they pay their franchisor fees, is correct. By stipulating that franchisees must register for VAT from the outset and by requiring copies of the franchisees VAT returns provides a secondary check for the franchisor.

Franchisees will know that if they falsify their financial returns to the franchisor then they will also have to falsify their returns to HM Revenue & Customs. In a worse case scenario, franchisees caught falsifying their returns to their franchisor can result in the loss of their franchise with no financial compensation. If however a franchisee is found to have falsified their returns to HM Revenue & Customs the penalty is much higher, and can be imprisonment! Therefore franchisees are much less likely to try and falsify returns when they are VAT registered compared with being unregistered.

Data Protection

If your franchisee requires the franchise to handle personal information about individuals, such as personnel records, client records, details about service users, they will have a number of legal obligations to protect that information.

There are a number of different statutes covering data protection and privacy. The main law governing data protection is the Data Protection Act 1998. The Act states that all organisations in the UK must comply with the Data Protection Act. The Act refers to the processing of personal data by data controllers and outlines the data protection principles which must be followed. Individuals are entitled to compensation for damage and distress caused by the failure of a data controller to comply with the Act.

The register of data controllers is held by the Information Commissioner's Office, www.ico.gov.uk. The register contains the name and address of data controllers and a description of the type of processing they do. It is very easy and cheap to register as a Data Controller. Registration can be done online, and in 2010 the registration cost was just £35.

It is very important however to make sure that the data registration register covers everything that the franchisee may use the data for, as it is otherwise a criminal offence. On a positive note, there is no negative consequence of including areas that the franchisee may not currently undertake, so it's best to cover all possibilities.

Keeping basic customer data is permissible without being registered, however the data protection rules are complex with a maximum penalty of £500,000 for a serious breach, so for the sake of a few pounds I believe that it should be something that unless there are compelling reasons to the contrary, all franchisees are made to do.

Selling a Franchise

One of the core elements that makes a business model a franchise rather than another expansion model, is that the franchisee owns their business and has the right to sell it. Clearly as a franchisor you will want to vet any person who wants to buy the franchise, however the business is ultimately an asset owned by the franchisee which they can sell.

There are many reasons why franchisees look to sell

There are many reasons why franchisees look to sell. These may range from health issues for the franchisee, the franchisee has grown the business and they want to realise the value of the business, or just that the franchisee wants to move on to something else or maybe wants to retire. It is therefore essential that the conditions surrounding a franchisee selling the business are stipulated at the outset.

Most franchisors make it a condition that they have the first right to buy the franchise back, even if the franchisee has identified a purchaser. In these cases it is important for the protection of the franchisee's asset that there are conditions in place covering what the franchisor must pay. The usual condition is that the franchisor must match the other purchaser's offer, so long as it is a genuine offer and not one instigated by the franchisee just to inflate the price the franchisor must pay!

Franchise sales should not be viewed as necessarily a bad thing. Franchise sales back to the franchisor can be of strategic benefit to the franchisor where for instance they may wish to increase the number of company owned outlets. Franchise sales to new franchise owners can bring a new impetus and vigour to the franchised business, which is often the case where a franchisee has run their business for many years and either doesn't want to grow their business further or has lost enthusiasm.

It is becoming more common that the topic of franchise sales is discussed with prospective franchisees at the interview stage before they even become franchisees. If successful, franchise sales are a natural inevitability for the franchisor.

Franchise Renewals

In most cases, regardless as to the actual length of the initial franchise term, franchises usually offer the franchisee an option to renew. The renewal terms vary greatly between franchises. Some franchises offer the franchisee one right to renew, for the same duration as their initial franchise, after which they have no right to renew again. Therefore a franchise may have a 5 year franchise with the right to renew for another 5 years, giving a total length of 10 years. Some franchises offer the franchisee the right to renew twice but on a different length to the initial term. In this example a franchise may be granted for 10 years with the option to renew for two periods of 5 years each, or the initial franchise may be 7 years with the option to renew for two periods of 5 years each.

Whatever renewal lengths are offered, usually the franchisee is not expected to pay the initial franchise fee again. It is not unusually however; for franchisees to be made to pay the franchisor's legal costs associated with the renewal.

The franchisee must renew their franchise on the terms of the Franchise Agreement currently being offered to new franchisees

An almost universal element of a franchise renewal is that the franchisee must renew their franchise on the terms of the Franchise Agreement currently being offered to new franchisees, at the time of renewal. This ensures that as many franchisees within a network are on the same Agreement and that any changes that have occurred with the Franchise Agreement over the initial term, which could be 5, 7, 10 years or more, will apply to any renewal franchise.

Another very common clause is that the franchisee must upgrade their equipment, or in the case of a premises based franchise, redecorate and replace equipment, so that it is of the standard and condition suitable for a new franchise.

It is important at this stage to address the issue as to whether renewal is down to the franchisee or whether the franchisor has a choice to renew or not. In most cases the franchisor must renew the franchise if the franchisee requests it. However; virtually all Franchise Agreements will make it a condition of renewal that the franchisee has not been in material breach of their Franchise Agreement at any time during their franchise. This ensures that if a franchisee is not meeting all the requirements as laid down in the Franchise Agreement and the Franchise Operations Manual, the franchisor is not obliged to renew the franchise. This often occurs when a franchisor has decided that despite the failings of a franchisee, it is more beneficial to keep the franchisee trading rather than go through the process of terminating the franchise and either finding a replacement franchisee or having to run the franchise with franchisor staff.

The implications of franchise renewals are that when a franchisee buys a franchise they are usually committing to a long time in the business. Equally, from the franchisor's perspective, they must understand that if they sell franchises, they have a responsibility to manage and support their franchisees for a long period of time. Franchising for both franchisees and franchisors is a long term commitment.

Franchisee Premises

For many franchises the issue of what type of premises the franchise will operate from is not open for debate. A restaurant franchise has to be operated from commercial premises with A3 permission, whereas a retail shop franchise has to operate from commercial premises with A1 permission.

However; there are many franchises that are specifically designed to be run from the franchisee's home without the need for commercial premises. In these cases it is important that the franchisee informs all relevant bodies, such as their landlord or mortgage company, their insurance provider, and the local authority.

For a number of franchises the decision is less clear cut. There are obvious advantages from having a franchisee work from home, most notably because it is much cheaper than taking on commercial premises. However this has to be balanced with the effect it may have on the franchisee's customers. If a franchise requires customers to meet them at the franchisees place of work, will working from home be seen as less professional to the customer? The franchisor also needs to consider how the franchise brand will be perceived by the public if all their franchisees work from home.

Again as with most elements of a franchise there is no right or wrong answer. The franchise must be developed to suit the individual franchise business. This is where many businesses fail by choosing to franchise their business using template franchise models that they download from the internet or are offered by some consultants. To stand the best chance of having a successful franchise business it is essential that every element of the franchise is developed to meet the specific needs and traits of that business.

Franchise Territories

Exclusive or not exclusive that is the question? Opinion is divided when it comes to franchise territories. The majority of franchises sell exclusive territories. This is where the franchisee is given a specific defined territory, normally geographically defined, that no other franchise can proactive market in. This allows the franchisee to get maximum benefit from their area without the risk of competition from within their franchise network. However, there are a number of franchises, a large

Exclusive or not exclusive?

percentage of which are very well established large franchise networks that have moved to non exclusive territories. These franchisors have moved to a non exclusive territory model as the customer demand is so high for their products or services that limiting the number of franchised outlets would result in demand not being met. Franchisees that buy these non exclusive territory franchises do so because the brand is so well known they can still be successful even with other competing outlets close by, a good example of this would be McDonalds.

If you are planning to offer exclusive territory franchises, which on the whole I think work better, it is important to be scientific about the way the territory criteria is developed. Franchising is all about following a proven model. Therefore if a business generates a £100,000 profit from within a certain catchment area with a specific number of potential customers, a franchise will have to have a similar catchment area with similar numbers of potential customers if they are going to make a £100,000 profit. Too often, not enough care is taken when creating franchise territory criteria. I know of a lawn care franchise that has a territory criteria based on the number of households. This is slightly better than purely being based on population however what happens when the franchise territory is an inner city area with a high proportion of flats? Just because there are a certain number of household in a given area doesn't mean they all have lawns! For this type of franchise it would be much more sensible to set the criteria based on the number of houses with gardens. Alternatively, if you have a business that sells predominately to women of a certain age then your franchise territory criteria should be based around territories having a certain number of women within the desired age range. By offering exclusive territory franchises based on a minimum number of target customers will give your franchisees the best chance for success.

National and Key Accounts

The question often raised by businesses looking to franchise is regarding what will happen with the national and key customers when they franchise. The company may have established a really good relationship with the customer and doesn't want to give these over to a franchisee. It may also be that the customer does not want to change who they deal with. It is therefore important that consideration is given in the Franchise Development Model as to what the policy will be regarding key and national accounts.

In regards to key accounts, the franchisor needs to take a pragmatic approach. It is not practical to sell a franchise with an exclusive customer and then inform the franchisee that the best customers are the franchisor's key accounts and will remain with the franchisor. Whilst this may be good for the franchisor, the franchisee could be left with a territory that has poor potential. Conversely the franchisor will not want to give away all their key customers to a franchisee. This is where common sense for both parties should prevail.

The franchisor must only nominate key account customers where there is a real risk that changing the person who deals with the customer could result in the business being lost altogether.

The franchisee has to be realistic about the need for certain customers to stay with the franchisor, as it is in the interest of the franchisee that the franchisor can run a profitable core business.

It may be that the franchisor and franchisee need to work together in the short term to ensure that any customers passed to the franchisee are happy with the change, and if the franchise model is based on an ongoing franchisor fee structure linked to the franchisee's turnover, then it is in the interest of both to work together to keep the business.

Many businesses have customers that have operations across the country. For these national customers it is perfectly reasonable for the franchisor to identify these as National Accounts. A national account therefore can be defined as any customer that has outlets in more than one franchisee territory. It is likely that the customer will only want to deal with one contact rather than lots of individual franchisees. Therefore with all national accounts, the franchisor is the contact that deals with the customer. The franchisor decides and agrees the terms with the customer and allows their franchises to deliver on the contract in their own territory. Alternatively the franchisor can decide to deliver on the contract themselves, in each of the franchisees territory.

In a number of franchises, national accounts can make up a large proportion of the franchisee's business. The franchisee may not make as much money from these national account customers as often the franchisor will have offered preferential rates to secure the business, however the benefit to the franchisee is that they have not had to do anything to get the business. I have seen problems arise where the franchisor has secured a national account but on terms that make it financial unviable for the franchisee, and despite this the franchisor insists the franchisee takes the business for the overall benefit of the brand. As with every aspect of franchising, the same principles apply; if a franchise is to be successful it must work for both franchisor and franchisee. As soon as one party feels that it isn't working, the franchise will fail.

> *For a franchise to be successful it must work for both the franchisor and franchisee*

Training

Given that franchising is all about a franchisee following the franchisor's systems, processes and business model exactly, a key aspect of the franchise package will be the training of the franchisee. The franchisee will need to be trained in every relevant aspect of the business so that they can replicate the franchisors model. The franchisee will need to be trained on how to run a business and how to deliver and/or sell the services or products in strict accordance with the Operations Manual.

No matter how good the initial franchisee training is, it is inevitable that franchisee will not remember everything. That is why it is essential that the franchisee has a really detailed Operations Manual that covers every aspect of the business in absolute detail. In addition, there are occasions where a franchisee will need additional training. This may be because the franchisor has launched a new product or service which the franchisee will need to sell, or it could be that despite having an Operations Manual they need a personal refresher course.

Often when the franchisor launches new products or services they will run a training course that the franchisor will fund themselves. The franchisee then only has to pay for their own travel and expenses. However, where the franchisee has already been trained but still needs additional training, it is normal that the franchisor will charge the franchisee for this training.

It is my belief that it is correct that a franchisor should be able to enforce additional training for their franchisees, where the franchisor believes that the franchisee is failing in part of their business. This additional training should be charged to the franchisee. Often, Franchise Agreements just state that the franchisor can insist that the franchisee attends additional training at the franchisee's cost. Where there is no limit on the number of days training and/or the cost of the training is not specified, it leaves the whole area of additional training open for potential abuse. A franchisor who is not happy with a franchisee could insist a franchisee attends training 2 days a week, every week of the year, and charge the franchisee £10,000 a day for the training! Of course in reality these extremes will not happen, however the franchisor is expecting a franchisee to sign the Franchise Agreement, which is a legally binding document that has no

A franchisor should be able to enforce additional training for their franchisees

protection in it against this type of abuse. If a franchisor says that they would never force a franchisee to do an unreasonable amount of additional training or training at an unreasonable rate, then I think it is perfectly reasonable for the franchisor to state what they think is reasonable, such as up to 5 days training a year at no more than £500 per day when delivered internally or at cost when delivered by external trainers.

In many franchises, the franchisee will employ staff. The question then is who should undertake franchisee staff training? There are no strict rules as to who delivers the training as every franchise is different. If the franchisee is employing salespeople who will be meeting customers and selling under the franchisor's brand, it would not be unreasonable for the franchisor to insist that all salespeople should be either trained by the franchisor or trained by the franchisee but accredited by the franchisor before they can be customer facing. Where the franchisee will need office staff that do not have direct dealing with customers then it may be totally reasonable for the franchisee to train these staff themselves with no involvement or accreditation from the franchisor.

In situations where customer facing staff are required from the start of the franchisees business, often staff training is undertaken by the franchisor as part of the initial Franchise Fee and therefore there is no additional cost to the franchisee. However, where the franchisee takes on additional staff or replaces staff that will need training, it would be usual for the franchisee to pay for this training. As with the ongoing franchisee training it is important that the franchisee is clear at the outset what the costs of additional staff training will be.

The cost in providing training may vary from year to year, just as any price may change from year to year. Therefore it is usual that the price of training is not stated in the Franchise Agreement but that the Franchise Agreement refers to a Training Price Tariff which is listed in the Operations Manual. If the prices are listed in the Operations Manual it allows the franchisor to amend them as required without the need to reissue the Franchise Agreement.

Death or Incapacity

Not wishing to end this chapter on a gloomy note, consideration does need to be given as to what happens if the franchisee becomes long term ill, incapacitated or worse still dies.

If a franchisee becomes ill and unable to work for any length of time there may be a real impact on the franchisees business. If the franchisor charges a percentage of turnover as an ongoing fee then the franchisor's income may be greatly reduced. If the franchisor charges a fixed amount each month then the franchisee may not be able to pay it. In these cases it is normal that the franchisor is able to put a qualified person into the franchisee's business to run it for them until the franchisee recovers. This ensures that the franchisee's business does not fail and keeps the income stream for the franchisor. Where a person is put in to run a franchisee's business it is usual for the franchisee to pay the manager's salary and expenses.

So what happens if the franchisee does not get better or something happens that permanently prevents them from running their franchise? In this case a qualified person should be supplied by the franchisor to run the franchises business until it is either sold to another franchisee or the franchisor buys the franchise themselves. When developing the Franchise Model, consideration needs to be given as to the length of time that it is reasonable to give the franchisee to sell their business and what happens if after this time the franchise hasn't been sold.

Lastly consideration needs to be given as to what will happen in the event of the death of a franchisee. As a franchisee owns their business the beneficiaries of the franchisee will have the issue of deciding what to do with the franchise. The options open to them are likely to be: operate the franchise themselves, find someone else to operate it, or sell it.

If the beneficiaries want to operate the franchise themselves or find someone else to run the franchise for them, then it is essential that the franchisor has the right to ensure that the person who will run the franchise is suitable. Where the person is not suitable the franchisor has the right to veto their appointment. Where the person is suitable it is very likely that they will need training, which the franchisor has a right to charge for.

Where the beneficiaries decides to sell the franchise then they will need to be given a reasonable time to find a buyer. As with dealing with franchisee incapacity it is important that consideration has been given to what would be a reasonable time for the beneficiaries to make the decision as to what they want to do with the franchise and the length of time after the decision has been taken for it to take place.

Chapter 4

THE FRANCHISE DEVELOPMENT MODEL - PART 3

The final parts of the Franchise Development Model are concerned with:

- The Role of the Franchisee and the Franchisor
- The Franchisee Profile
- The Financial Projections for both the Franchisee and Franchisor
- The Obligations for both the Franchisee and Franchisor

The Role of the Franchisee and the Franchisor

When developing a franchise model it is critical to identify the roles and responsibilities for both the franchisor and franchisees. A franchisor needs to be clear about what franchisees are responsible for and how they support them.

One of the biggest mistakes that people make when developing their franchise is to expect the franchisee to do everything. Most franchisees do not have extensive business experience and this means that they will not have the skills and experience to competently undertake every aspect of their franchise. If we look at the typical one person run franchise, is it reasonable to expect the franchisee to be an expert marketer, an expert sales person, an expert service deliverer, an expert bookkeeper, and an expert research and developer? The reason most people choose to become a franchisee is because they do not have the skills or expertise to set-up and run their own business. Even with the most detailed and comprehensive Franchise Operations Manual it is unreasonable to expect a franchisee to be able to be an expert in all parts of their business. In most franchises, the most important role for a franchisee is sales. Without customers the franchisee will not have a business. If a franchisor can undertake as many aspects of the business that they can it will enable a franchisee to spend more of their time generating sales. The more sales a franchisee makes, the more profitable they will be and the more money

Do not expect franchisees to do everything

a franchisor will make from their management fees or mark-up on products.

Undertaking elements of a franchisee's business for them has the added benefit for the franchisor in that they can control the way these elements of the business are run. The franchisor will charge the franchisee for these services and is likely to benefit from economy of scale by undertaking these roles throughout their franchisee network.

The one area of the business that I would advise franchisors not to take ownership of, unless there are very good reasons, would be local marketing. After the initial Launch Marketing Campaign which I recommend franchisors handle, I believe franchisees must take responsibility for their own local marketing, otherwise there is a real risk that franchisees may sit back and wait for business to happen. If all marketing were to be handled by the franchisor, there is a real possibility that as soon as the level of customer leads fall below the franchisee's expectations, they will be unhappy. The last thing franchisors want is for franchisees to start complaining or worse still take legal action, if the franchisees business starts to underperform or fail.

The Franchisee Profile

Having worked out the roles and responsibilities for the franchisee and franchisor it is important to identify what type of person would be suitable for the franchise and what type of experience and background they require.

Type of Person

The type of person who will be suited as a franchisee depends totally on what they will be expected to do within their franchise. Will the franchisee be selling jams and chutneys to customers on a market stall; will the franchisee be selling advertising space for a community magazine over the phone; or will the franchisee be selling bookkeeping services to owners or managing directors of companies? In each of these three examples the personality and type of person suited to the franchisee role will be very different. Clearly someone with a quiet reserved personality is likely to be unsuitable to sell on a market stall, someone who lacks confidence may be totally unsuitable for telephone cold calling, yet someone with a very exuberant character may well be suitable to sell professional services such as bookkeeping to business owners. Personality traits are something that is very difficult to change in people and it is not the remit of a franchisor. Therefore it is important to be absolutely clear about the type of person suited to the role of the franchisee.

Background and Experience

Some franchises, despite having a detailed Franchise Operations Manual, will require their franchisees to have prior experience. This experience may be in selling and dealing with the type of customers they will have in their franchise, or it may be that they need a basic understanding in a certain area such as being able to drive, if it's a delivery franchise or an understanding of computers if they are going to run a PC repair franchise.

On the other hand some franchisors do not want their franchisees to have too much prior experience in the area of the franchise as there is a real risk that despite the franchisee saying at interview that they will follow all the franchisor's systems and processes exactly, that once they start operating their franchise, they fall back to the ways they may have worked in the past. By taking franchisees with little or no prior experience prevents this from happening as they do not have any past experience to fall back on.

Appropriateness

On a serious but slightly light hearted note, it is important that the franchisee has to have the appropriate qualities for the role they will have to undertake and a degree of common sense needs to come into play. If you have a roof repair franchise which requires the franchisee to work at heights then it is important to ensure that franchisees do not suffer from vertigo and are fit enough to undertake the role. If a franchise involves selling pet food directly to customer's homes, it will be no good if a franchisee has an allergy to animals as it is likely that they will come into contact with them in their line of business. I have known of someone who wanted to buy a lawn care franchise but hadn't realised that they would have to work with machinery as they had a bad back and couldn't do any lifting and operation of heavy equipment! It is easy to think that nobody would apply for a franchisee that they wouldn't be suitable for, however experience shows this isn't always the case, so the message to all franchisors is to make sure you ask the relevant questions at the interview stage, however obvious they may seem!

Financial Projections

When developing the franchise model it is critical that financial projections are undertaken both for the franchisee and the franchisor to ensure that the model works for both parties.

The Franchisee

Although no two franchisees, even in the same franchise, will perform exactly the same, it is important to work out conservative financial projections that every franchisee can reasonably be expected to achieve. There is a temptation to inflate these financial projections so that franchisors can make marvellous earning claims in their franchisee recruitment material, however financial projections must be realistic.

Previously we have looked at the type of person who becomes a franchisee and seen that on the whole they are not entrepreneurs or the top salespeople in the country.

Franchisees are normally average people who on the whole will operate to an average standard. Some franchisees will be brilliant and exceed all expectations, but some franchisees, despite careful interviewing and ongoing support will always struggle. Therefore when creating franchisee projections I prefer to err on the side of caution on the basis that it is far better for people to exceed their projections than to fail to achieve them. Franchisees that exceed the projections will inevitably be happy, motivated and sing the praises of the franchise. This is good for the morale of franchisees, and happy franchisees are much easier to manage, and will help with your future franchisee recruitment.

Be conservative when creating franchisee projections

Many prospective franchisees will ask to speak to existing franchisees, and what better way of convincing a prospective franchisee about the franchise, than to have franchisees singing the praises of the franchise!

When it comes to providing franchisees with financial projections it is important to tailor them to fit their own circumstances. It may be that there is more competition in their territory than others, which will mean that their speed of growth may be slower than for other franchisees. It may be that the competitors have very aggressive pricing policies which may mean that the franchisee has to reduce their prices to compete. If the franchisee employs staff it may be that the franchise is in a part of the country where the wages are higher than in other areas, or it may be that the franchise operates from retail premises and the cost of getting suitable premises and the associated rent and rates are higher than in other parts of the country. All of these factors and many more are critical factors that the franchisee must consider and accordingly amend the franchise projections provided by the franchisor, to accurately reflect their own personal circumstances.

It is also worth considering that if a franchisee needs to borrow to finance their franchise, it is likely that they will approach a Bank. Banks will expect to see a business plan specifically tailored to the franchisee's own circumstances. Banks do not like to see franchisees presenting a template business plan that has been created by the franchisor and which is the same for every franchisee in their network. Not only do they immediately know it is unlikely to be representative of the franchisee's own business but also it shows a lack of professionalism on the part of the franchisee. Franchisors should help the franchisee with their business plan but ultimately it is the franchisee's responsibility for ensuring that it is a realistic representation of what will happen in their own territory.

Franchisor Projections

I have often heard business owners question the need to create franchisor projections, believing that they only need to create franchisee projections as they are only selling to franchisees. Often in an attempt to make the Franchise Package as attractive as possible, a franchisor forgets the impact on their own business. I have seen a franchisor who charged a fixed £500 a month management fee, however the franchisor was spending a day a month with each of their franchisees in the franchisees own territory. The franchisor was also doing the bookkeeping for their franchisees whilst also researching and developing new products and services for their franchise network. You don't need to have a degree in mathematics to work out that the franchisor only makes £6,000 a year from each franchisee whilst in return they were spending 12 days a year with each franchisee, doing the bookkeeping and spending time and money researching and developing new products. The cost for undertaking only these elements, without taking into account the cost of the head office staff, head office premises and operating costs was far more per franchisee than the £6,000 they received from each franchisee! This clearly does not make commercial sense and there is a real risk that either the franchisor will become bankrupt or will fail to deliver on everything the franchisee expects and needs.

There are other franchisors whose financial projections only start to work when certain levels of franchisee recruitment are achieved. Some franchisors base their financial projections on totally unrealistic recruitment levels. I have heard business owners stating that they are going to recruit 50 franchisees in year one, 100 in year two and 200 in year three! Clearly nothing is impossible however to recruit one franchisee a week in the first year, two franchisees a week in year two and four franchisees a week in year three is not only virtually unheard of, but clearly the resources required to recruit, train, launch and support such large numbers of

Some franchisors base their financial projections on totally unrealistic recruitment levels

franchisees would be enormous. In my experience for most new franchisors, if they recruit 4 to 6 franchisees in their first year they would be doing quite well; and if they recruit 6 to 8 in year two and the same in year three, this would be above average.

It is far better when considering the profitability of a franchise model to work on conservative franchisee recruitment levels. If the model still works at conservative levels then if the franchisor exceeds these levels, it can only work in their favour. For franchising to work, the franchise model must show it being financially profitable for both franchisee and franchisor.

Obligations

One of the final considerations, when creating the Franchise Package, is to state the obligations for the franchisee and the franchisor.

Franchisee obligations

Many franchisee obligations may seem obvious, however to avoid any confusion and difficulties in the future it is far better to state them at the outset. Typically franchisee obligations would include:

- To pay the franchisor in an accurate and timely manner.
- To operate in strict accordance with the Franchise Operations Manual.
- To uphold the confidentiality of all aspects of the franchisor's and franchisee's business.
- To ensure that all staff are trained to the level required to competently operate within the business.
- Not to do anything that will bring the franchisor or the franchisor's brand into to disrepute.
- To take all reasonable steps to realise the potential of their business in their territory.
- To attend all franchisee meetings, conferences and training sessions.

Franchisor obligations

I have stated on a number of occasions that franchising only works when it works for both parties. Therefore if there are obligations on the franchisee, it is only reasonable to expect that there should be obligations on the franchisor. Typically franchisor obligations would include:

- To train the franchisee so that they are competent to successfully run their franchised business.
- To help the franchisee set-up and launch their business.
- To provide ongoing support and advice in a timely manner.
- To research and develop products and services for their franchisees to ensure that the franchisee's business remains competitive in their marketplace.
- To take all reasonable steps to protect the franchisee's business.
- To protect the franchisor's brand and reputation.
- To take quick and incisive action to stop any unsuitable action by franchisees within their network.

The Franchise Development Model - Summary

This section highlights the various areas for prospective franchisor's to consider when developing a Franchise Model:

- The Franchise Package
- The Terms of the Franchise
- The Role of the Franchisee and the Franchisor
- The Franchisee Profile
- The Financial Projections for both Franchisee and Franchisor

- The Obligations for both Franchisee and Franchisor

Some business owners may question whether all this planning is really necessary and want to just get going with franchising their business. If the Franchise Development Model is right, it will be used as the blueprint for all other areas of the franchise development and will give the franchisor the best chance for success.

The Franchise Development Model is the blueprint for all other areas of the franchise development

If not enough time is spent on the Franchise Development Model, or elements are not in enough detail, there is a real chance that the franchisor will experience problems. Some people may say that this is a risk worth taking however; I believe that if a franchisor is taking a franchisee's money, they have a legal obligation to do everything reasonable to ensure the franchisee is successful, and they definitely have in my view a morale obligation to protect the franchisee's investment.

Sometimes having gone through the Franchise Development Model phase, a business owner will decide not to go forward with franchising. Not because it may not be financially viable but simply because they didn't realise the full implications of franchising done properly. In these cases the time and money spent on doing the Franchise Development Model can be the best time and money spent as it can flag up the issues with franchising and allow consideration of other more suitable expansion models.

SECTION 2

Infrastructure Development

Section Two will look at what needs to be done, once a business has created their Franchise Development Model and decided that they are going to franchise their business, before they will be ready to start marketing the franchise opportunity.

This section has been split into four chapters:

Chapter 5 - **Systems & Process Development**
This will cover the various internal systems and processes that may be required to successfully manage a franchise network.

Chapter 6 - **Franchise Legal Documents**
This will cover the main legal documents required when setting up a franchise, recruiting franchisees, and the ongoing running and management of a franchise network.

Chapter 7 - **Franchise Operations Manual**
This will discuss what the objective of the Franchise Operations Manual should be, the types of information it should contain, and how it should be used.

Chapter 8 - **Other Development Areas**
The final chapter in this section will cover three other development areas that need to be addressed before you can consider your franchisee recruitment. These areas include how to create a franchisee training

programme, developing a franchise business plan that can be tailored and personalised by each franchisee, and lastly how to create franchise territories.

Chapter 5

SYSTEMS & PROCESS DEVELOPMENT

Franchisors must ensure that they have all the systems and processes necessary to run and manage a network of franchisees. These systems and processes can be split into two categories:

1. Head Office Systems
2. Franchise Operating Systems.

Head Office Systems

These are the head office systems and processes that are required to carry out the role of franchisor. If a business operates from a single site then it may be that the systems and processes that they currently use work well now but may need upgrading or changing if they are going to be used by franchisees operating from multiple locations.

Most companies have systems and processes in place to record customer information and data. It will be essential that this is reviewed to see whether it has both the capacity to store the volume of customer data that may be generated by the franchisees and that it can be accessed and used remotely by franchisees.

Another consideration when it comes to the storing of customer data relates to where the data will be stored. It is usually much better for franchisors if data is stored centrally with them rather than stored locally in each franchisees own computer. Storing customer data centrally will make it easier to ensure that the data is regularly backed up in case of loss or corruption of data. Storing data centrally also provides franchisors with an additional level of control against franchisees setting up in competition with an existing database of customers. The Franchise Agreement usually states that when a franchisee is terminated or no longer active, that all the customer data reverts to the franchisor. If the franchisor already stores the customer data centrally, this is easier to enforce than if the franchisor has to retrieve the customer data from a franchisee.

Another area to consider is how to communicate with franchisees. It may be easy to communicate with staff based all in the same place, but will the same communication processes be as effective with a network of franchisees based different parts of the country? For many franchisors effective communication with a franchisee network will often require a more structured approach to communication than is required for communicating in a single office.

I have highlighted a few areas that need to be considered when assessing whether existing head office systems and processes are suitable for use by a network of franchisees. Every business is different and therefore companies considering franchising must undertake a review of all their head office systems and processes, and where necessary make changes before launching their franchise.

Franchise Operating Systems

Before franchisees are recruited, a review of all systems and processes relating to the sales and delivery of the products and services of the business will be required. A pet food delivery business will need to review their existing systems and process to assess suitability for use by franchisees covering areas such as: how will franchisees order stock, how will the stock be delivered, how will franchisees deliver orders to their customers, how will customers pay, how will internet orders be processed and delivered. It may be that currently delivery staff collect all customer orders direct from a central warehouse, however would this be practical for a franchisee based at the other end of the country?

It may be that customers phone orders to a central telephone number, and the order is sent to the warehouse for processing, after which delivery is scheduled. How is this process going to work with a network of nationwide franchisees? Consideration will need to be given as to whether to keep one central telephone order number or for each franchisee to have their own local order number. If one central number is kept then systems and processes will be required to ensure local franchisees are aware of their customer orders. If franchisees have separate local numbers, new systems and processes will be required to ensure a central record of customer orders is maintained and correct stock levels can be maintained centrally.

These operational issues may be relatively easy to sort out, however as with the head office systems and processes, careful consideration of all these issues is required before franchisees are recruited.

Pilot Operation

I am often asked whether it is essential for a business to run a pilot before launching a franchise; however I can give no definite answer. As previously stated franchising is based on the concept of a franchisee buying and operating a "proven" business model. The question that prospective franchisors need to ask is whether there is sufficient proof that their business will be successful in different parts of the country, when delivered by a network of franchisees.

Often, products or services that are popular in one part of the country and not as popular other parts of the country.

Franchising is based on the concept of a franchisee buying and operating a "proven" business model

How will a prospective franchisor know this about their products and services? This may be easy to answer if the business has a client database which includes both local and national customers, but what happens if all the customers are local?

If a business does not have offices or outlets around the country, it may be that one or two pilot operations will be required first to prove that the demand exists. Often however, a business can point to competitors that sell similar products and services throughout the country, for their proof. If one takes a take away pizza business, is it really necessary to set up one or two pilot stores around the country to prove that people buy take away pizzas? The question of proof then changes to the question of demand and whether it exists and whether it can be operated successfully in different locations. This comes back to whether the systems and processes are in place to support a nationwide network.

One of the reasons for running a pilot, even if there is proof that demand does exist nationwide and that the systems and process are in place to support a nationwide network of franchisees, is to provide additional proof of the brands success to prospective franchisees. The reason many people choose to become franchisees is because they feel that start their own business would be too risky. Consequently many franchisees are cautious and risk adverse. Clearly for risk adverse prospective franchisees, a business that has successfully operated in different parts of the country will give much more comfort than a business that has only operated in one location. Basically the more proof of success that can be provided to a prospective franchisee the better.

In conclusion, business owners need to understand the extent and cost of any developments required to their systems and processes before they make a final decision as to whether to franchise their business or not. They also need to weigh up the pros and cons of setting up a pilot operation if they only operate in one location. Strategically it may be better to accept that franchise recruitment will be harder without having run any pilot operations rather than spend the time and money setting up a pilot. There are no laws in the UK that states a pilot operation has to be run before a company can franchise, therefore the final decision on whether to pilot or not is down to each business owner.

Chapter 6

FRANCHISE LEGAL DOCUMENTS

As franchising is a legal contract between the franchisor and the franchisee, there needs to be a legal document setting out the conditions under which the franchisee is buying the franchise, the obligations of both franchisor and franchisee and what happens if any of these conditions or obligations are broken. It is for this reason that franchisees are required to sign a "Franchise Agreement". However, depending on the way the franchise is structured, there will be a number of other legal documents that are required. The main legal documents in franchising are:

- Confidentiality Agreement
- Deposit Agreement
- Franchise Agreement
- Commercial Lease Agreement

- Software License Agreement
- Intellectual Property Assignment Rights
- Employment Contracts
- Telephone Transfer Agreement

There is also one other key legal process that a franchisor needs to consider, Trade Marking.

Confidentiality Agreement

If a person is going to buy a franchise, it is not surprising that a franchisor will have to provide the prospective franchisee with large amounts information about the business and how it operates, much of which will be confidential information. Without providing this confidential information it will be virtually impossible for a prospective franchisee to make an informed decision as to whether the franchise is right for them. So how does a franchisor prevent a prospective franchisee from taking all the information they are given and either set up in direct competition using this information or pass the information to a competitor? To prevent this franchisees are required to sign a Confidentiality Agreement BEFORE any information is given to them that the company would not want to get in to the public domain.

The Confidentiality Agreement is a legally binding document the prospective franchisee signs to say that the franchisor will be providing them with confidential information which they may only use for the purpose of deciding whether to become a franchisee or not. The prospective franchisee is also signing to say that they will not share any confidential information with any other person without the franchisor's express written permission.

If a prospective franchisee wishes to bring a spouse or friend with them to any meeting where confidential information will be provided, it is important to ensure that separate Confidentiality Agreements are signed by every person present, not just the prospective franchisee.

Ensure that separate Confidentiality Agreements are signed by every person present

Deposit Agreement

Having received signed Confidentiality Agreements from all relevant parties, it is safe for the franchisor to provide all the information that a prospective franchisee will need to decide whether to buy the franchise. If having provided all the relevant information and answered all the prospective franchisee's questions the franchisor wants to offer them a franchise, what happens next?

Firstly the franchisor will need to formally offer them the opportunity to become a franchisee. If they want to accept the offer ultimately they will need to sign the Franchise Agreement. However, before providing someone with a

Franchise Agreement, many franchisors require something more concrete than just an acknowledgement that the individual is interested in purchasing the franchise. This is because until the Franchise Agreement is signed there is nothing binding the individual to go through with the purchase of the franchise. On many occasions, franchisors can spend considerable amounts of time answering questions, particularly on the finer details of the Franchise Agreement, only to find at the last moment the person pulls out. A franchisor may have turned down other enquiries for the franchise territory since they were already in meaningful discussion with a prospective franchisee, only to find out the prospective franchisee decides not to proceed and the second person who enquired has moved on and bought a different franchise. One way to help assess the level of commitment of a prospective franchisee is to require them to put down a deposit to "ring fence" the territory whilst they review the Franchise Agreement. A deposit will provide the prospective franchisee with confidence that, for a set period of time, the franchisor will not take forward any other enquiries for the specific franchise territory in question. A deposit also gives the franchisor confidence that if a prospective franchisee has paid a deposit they are more likely to be serious about buying the franchise.

As a prospective franchisee is making a payment to a franchisor there will need to be an acknowledgement from the franchisor that the deposit money has been paid and what conditions apply to the deposit, such as: is it fully refundable; can the franchisor deduct reasonable costs if the prospective franchisee pulls out; and what the deposit is for. All this information is contained within the Franchise Deposit Agreement. The prospective franchisee signs the Deposit Agreement and pays their deposit. The franchisor can then the Franchise Agreement to the prospective franchisee, with greater confidence.

Franchise Agreement

The Franchise Agreement is the most important document in the whole franchise process, as it lists the terms on which the franchise is offered, the obligations for both franchisor and franchisee, and most importantly what happens if something goes wrong. The Franchise Agreement then becomes a legally binding document for both franchisee and franchisor.

The Franchise Agreement is the most important document in the whole franchise process

Most professionally drawn up Franchise Agreements are about 50 pages long. Many business owners new to franchising question whether the Franchise Agreement has to be so long, fearing that the length may put off prospective franchisees. Not unsurprisingly, there is good reason why Franchise Agreements are this length and that isn't just to justify solicitor's fees! Over the years, when problems have arisen that were not covered adequately in Franchise

Agreements, solicitors added new clauses to prevent these problems reoccurring. This means that Franchise Agreements have a tendency to get longer each year, very rarely getting shorter!

It is very important that franchisors don't apologies for the length of their Franchise Agreement. Franchisors should explain to prospective franchisees that the Franchise Agreement needs to be that length to protect them both.

Franchise Agreements have a tendency to get longer each year, very rarely getting shorter!

Most franchise agreements follow a similar structure:

1. **Interpretation**
   This defines the meaning of key words or expressions used throughout the agreement

2. **Rights granted**
   This sets out what the rights of the franchisee are

3. **Terms and renewal**
   This states how long the franchise will be granted for and what happens at the end of the initial franchise term

4. **Franchisors obligations**
   This states what the franchisor will do for the

franchisee both in helping the franchisee set-up their business and then on an ongoing basis

5. *Franchisees obligations*

   This states what the franchisee must do during their franchise

6. *Training*

   This states whether the franchisor has the right to force a franchisee to attend additional training and if so under what conditions and who will pay for it

7. *Fees and payments*

   This states what fees the franchisee must pay and when

8. *Accounting*

   This states any specific conditions that the franchisee must follow with regards the franchisees accounting process and the records they must keep

9. *Marketing*

   This states what marketing a franchisee can do and any conditions surrounding it

10. *Insurance*

    This lists all the insurances that a franchisee must have and the level of cover for each

11. Trade mark

This stipulates the conditions under which the franchisee can use the franchisors Trade Marks

12. Sales of the business

This states the process the franchisee must follow if they want to sell the business and whether the franchisor will have the first right to buy the franchise back from the franchisee

13. Non-competition and confidentiality

This states that the franchisee must not set-up in competition with the franchisor and also that all information they are provided with by the franchisor must be kept confidential

14. Death or incapacity

This states the what should happen if the franchisee is unable to work for a period of time or dies

15. Minimum performance

This lists any minimum performance levels that a franchisee must meet and the consequences if they fail to achieve these minimum levels

16. Termination

This lists what happens if the franchisee has their franchise terminated by the franchisor, the key reasons why a franchise may be terminated, ad any post termination restrictions on the franchisee

17. *Improvements*

This states the policy regarding any improvements that the franchisor wishes to impose on the franchisee

18. *Operations manual*

This states that the Operations Manual forms part of the Franchise Agreement and that the franchisor may amend the Operations Manual at any time without having to reissue the Franchise Agreement

19. *Data protection*

This stipulates that the franchisee is responsible for complying with all Data Protection legislation

20. *National accounts*

This states the policy and process regarding national account business

21. *Other business formats*

This stipulates that the business is a franchise and is not an agency, trading scheme or any other type of business format

22. *Alternative dispute resolution*

This states what process will be followed if there is a dispute between the franchisor and the franchisee

23. *Jurisdiction*

This states under what country's law the Franchise Agreement is governed by.

As previously mentioned, every franchise business is different. Therefore it is essential that the Franchise Agreement is constructed to address the unique factors of that business. This means that there may be other sections in the Franchise Agreement that are required to cover areas which are specific to the franchisor's business.

It is for this reason that franchisors should be very wary about purchasing a Franchise Agreement template and filling in the blanks themselves. It is essential that business owners use the services of an accredited Franchise Solicitor as they will ensure that the Franchise Agreement is right for the business and protects the interest of both the franchisor and the franchisee.

Commercial Lease Agreement

Where a franchisee operates from a specific premises, and the location of the premises is critical to the success of the franchise, the franchisor may wish to take a "Lease Option" on the premises. The "Lease Option" gives the franchisor the right to take over the franchisee's lease if the franchisee loses their franchise i.e. the franchise is terminated.

A standard clause in Franchise Agreements gives the franchisor the right to take over a franchise and the franchisee's clients if the franchise is terminated. This is fine for franchises that do not operate from commercial premises or where the location of the premises is not critical to the business. However where the location of the premises is critical, the franchisor may want to take over the premises rather than finding a different one. This right to take over the premise is called an "Option". The lease signed by the franchisee will have a clause that stipulates, to the landlord, that they must, should the franchisor wish, assign the lease to the franchisor if the franchisee is no longer active.

Software License Agreement

Where the franchisor has developed bespoke software that is critical to the operation of the franchise, a software licence will be required. The software licence will grant the franchisee the right to use the software whilst they are a franchisee. Equally importantly, the software licence will stipulate that once no longer a franchisee, they do not have any right to use the software and must take all reasonable steps to ensure that any copies of the software and operating instructions are returned to the franchisor and that information about the structure and use of the software is kept confidential.

Employment Contracts

One of the reasons why businesses choose to franchise rather than expand through company owned expansion, are the concerns relating to both managing a large number of staff and all the associated employment legislation that it entails.

In many franchises, the franchisee will be required to employ staff. The franchisor has three options: 1) provide the franchisee with employment advice and all the employment forms they required; 2) leave all employment issues to the franchisee to deal with or 3) require the franchisee to use a professional outsourced employment service.

1. ***Provide the franchisee with employment advice and employment forms***

Unless the franchisor has staff that are specialists in employment law or outsources this, there is a real risk in trying to provide this type of advice to franchisees. If the franchisor provides incorrect advice or gives the franchisees employment forms that are out of date, the franchisor risks being sued by the franchisee should anything go wrong.

2. ***Leave all employment issues to the franchisee to deal with***

If a franchisor leaves a franchisee to deal with all aspects of staff employment, there is a real risk that the franchisee may make mistakes. The franchisor has to consider what the impact on the franchisor's brand and the rest of the franchisee network will be if the employment mistakes of one franchisee become public knowledge.

3. Make the franchisee use a professional outsourced employment service

In most cases, requiring the franchisee to use the services of a professional employment law and advisory company will ensure that the employment process and forms used by them comply with all employment legislation. This provides ultimate protection to the franchisor, the franchisee and the rest of the franchisee network, whilst also freeing up the franchisee's resources to focus on running their business.

Trade Marking

One of the core elements of a franchise is that the franchisor will grant the franchisee the right to operate under their company name and have use of the logo's and strap lines associated with it. This means that the franchisor must own the rights to the name, logo and strap lines if they are going to grant a franchisee the right to use them. This is achieved through a process called Trade Marking.

The only way to protect against another business operating under the same name is to Trade Mark it

Often business owners get confused between Trade Marking and other registrations such as Domain Registration or Company Formation. Just because a business owns a domain name it does not stop anyone setting up and operating a business using the same name. Domain registrations only prevent someone from using the exact same internet domain name, although they can use a domain name which is very similar. Company Formation again provides no protection against a company trading under the same name as someone else. Company Formation allows Companies House to identify businesses that are filing their accounts.

The only way to protect against another business operating under the same name is to Trade Mark it. This is a relatively straight forward process and can either be done online through the Intellectual Property Office or through many solicitors and Trade Mark Registration companies.

Intellectual Property Assignment Rights

It is very common for businesses that franchise to set-up a new company to run and manage the franchise from. Operating a franchise from a separate company provides many advantages to the franchisor however consideration needs to be given as to whether the franchisor company is the company that owns the Trade Marks of the business or the business owner.

In many cases the Trade Mark will have been registered in the name of one of the owners of the business or in the business name. In these cases an "Intellectual Property

Assignment" agreement will need to be produced which grants the new franchisor company the right to use the Trade Marks.

Telephone Transfer Agreement

One of the ways of making it difficult for a franchisee to set-up in competition with the franchisor, is to make sure that the franchisor has control over all the mediums which a customer can make contact with the franchisee. If a franchisee has an email address, it is important that the franchisor is the owner of the email address domain therefore emails can be diverted to the franchisor if the franchisee decides to leave and set-up in competition.

When it comes to telephones, faxes and mobiles, it is again important that the franchisor has controls in place to prevent the franchisee from continuing to use them when they are no longer a franchisee. This control is achieved either by the franchisor being the person who contracts to these services and then charges the franchisee to use them, or the franchisor leaves the franchisee to sign contracts for each of these services but with a Transfer Agreement attached to each.

A Transfer Agreement is signed by the franchisee and a copy is given to the phone or fax service provider, and a copy kept by the franchisor. The Transfer Agreement gives the franchisee's permission for the phone or fax to be transferred to the franchisor should they no longer be a franchisee. Although Transfer Agreements on their own will not prevent a franchisee from setting up in competition, it is one of many elements that will make it more difficult and inconvenient for a franchisee to go it alone.

Using Franchise Lawyers versus Template Legal Documents

Using specialist franchise legal advisers can be costly. Many business owners see companies on the internet selling template legal documents and agreements at a fraction of the price quoted by specialist franchise lawyers and question whether the extra expense is really necessary.

As previously indicated no two businesses are exactly the same. It is essential for the franchisor's business to have legal documents that are fit for purpose. To try and build a brand, nationally and/or

It is essential to have legal documents that are fit for purpose

internationally without the right protection in place is foolish. I believe that the franchisor has a legal and moral obligation to protect the investments of their franchisees. The only way to fully protect them is through having the right legal documents in place.

In my experience, I have also found that it is to the franchisees and franchisors advantage to use accredited franchise legal specialists rather than "general legal advisers". A list of all British Franchise Association specialist accredited franchise solicitors can be found on their website at www.thebfa.org/helpandadvice.

Chapter 7

FRANCHISE OPERATIONS MANUAL

The Franchise Operations Manual is one of the most critical parts of any franchise. The Franchise Operations Manual provides all the detailed instructions on how a franchisee must operate their business, and forms along with the Franchise Agreement, the legal conditions under which the franchisee will operate.

How much detail needs to be in a Franchise Operations Manual?

A common question I am often asked is how much detail needs to be in a Franchise Operations Manual? The answer is very straight forward, it is as detailed as it needs to be to ensure that every franchisee operates in exactly the same way. Unfortunately, most Franchise Operations Manuals I see have far too little detail. The defence often used by franchisors is that they want to treat their franchisees as adults and have them take ownership for their franchise they therefore want to leave certain elements up to each franchisee to decide. This is a major mistake. If you asked ten very sensible people to do the same task, it is very likely that they will do it in ten different ways. When a brand is at the mercy of its franchisees, there is a real risk that one or more of the franchisees may do something, which they think is very sensible, but which ultimate damages the franchisor's brand reputation. A franchisor has a responsibility to protect their franchisee's investments. The franchisee network will not be happy if the franchisor allows one franchisee to damage the brand which then ultimately affects the whole franchisee network.

The only way to ensure that every franchisee operates in exactly the same way is to leave nothing to interpretation. The Franchise Operations Manual has to state, in minute detail, exactly everything a franchisee should do and how they should do it.

As a Franchise Operations Manual needs to cover every part of the franchisee's business, and given that every business is slightly different, there is no such thing as a template Franchise Operations Manual. The only real use of a template Franchise Operations Manual is to give an idea of the topics to include.

Having said that every Franchise Operations Manual is different there are two distinct elements to the Manual: 1) setting up and running a franchised business 2) selling and delivering the products and services of the company.

Setting Up and Running a Franchised Business

Common areas included within this section of Franchise Operations Manual are:

1. Key contacts, when to contact them, and their contact details
2. A statement saying that the franchisor owns the copyright of the Franchise Operations Manual
3. How to use the Franchise Operations Manual and the process for its updating
4. What the franchisee needs to do when setting up their franchise, such as company formation, VAT registration, data protection registration, the different insurances they will require
5. Health & Safety compliance
6. Employing and managing staff
7. Training staff and ongoing franchisee training
8. Office layout, equipment and signage
9. Dress code policy
10. Vehicle type, livery, maintenance and usage
11. Telephone numbers, usage and policy

12. Email format and usage
13. Accounts and bookkeeping
14. Franchisee reporting requirements
15. Franchise territory rules
16. National accounts policy and procedure
17. The process for recommending improvements
18. Marketing policies
19. Marketing material available to franchisees
20. Local marketing policies
21. National marketing campaigns
22. Ordering branded products such as stationery and marketing material
23. Franchisor and franchisee website policies

In addition to providing detailed instructions for all the above, the Franchise Operations Manual will also need to contain copies of every form, document, template and guide that a franchisee may need to use.

Selling and Delivering Products and Services

This section of the Franchise Operations Manual will be different for each company. It will state in minute detail how the franchisee must sell and deliver their services and products. Typically it will cover all the usual stages in any customer sales transaction:

1. How to handle enquiries
2. What to do at customer meetings
3. Providing customer quotes
4. Processing customer orders
5. Taking customer payment
6. Delivering the service or product
7. Post sales follow up
8. What forms and documents to use
9. What levels of stock a franchisee should maintain
10. Customer complaints procedure

Most franchised business will have some form of computerised customer records system and within the Franchise Operations Manual, detailed instructions on how to enter information onto these computerised systems is required. Often franchisors will include screen prints of every step when entering information, as it is only through this level of detail and instructions can the franchisor be confident that the correct information will be entered in the correct place.

Another useful tool when creating this part of a Franchise Operations Manual is to include process flow charts for each stage of the sales process. Often flow charts are easier to follow than long paragraphs of text.

Online Manuals versus Hardcopy Manuals

Another question I am asked in relation to the Franchise Operations Manual is what should the format be, hardcopy or available online. I am from the old school view that many people prefer to have a hard copy Franchise Operations Manual rather than just using an online version. However there are pro's and con's for each approach.

An online version is easy to update centrally and allows a franchisee to access anywhere they can get internet access. The downside is that franchisees have a tendency to print off key sections of their online Franchise Operations Manual and do not replace sections as elements are changed and this means that they risk referring to out of date instructions.

Think about who is going to use the manual

A hard copy version makes it easier to ensure every Franchise Operations Manual is the same as each time there is a change a new page sent to the franchisee the franchisee is required to send a return to the franchisor acknowledging that they have read the new page and replaced the old page with the new one; however this is more time consuming for the franchisor. Another point to note is that Franchise Operations Manuals are large documents and can end up staying on a franchisees shelf as they are not always practical to carry around.

As modern technology continues to develop, I am sure that the days of hard copy Franchise Operations Manuals will be numbered. The best advice I can give is to think about who is going to use it. If the majority of franchisees are over 50 years of age then there may be an argument to use a hard copy format as the older the franchisee, the more comfortable they may be with a hard copy version. Conversely, if the franchisees are likely to be much younger, it is more likely that they will have grown up with technology and will feel more comfortable with an online version. Offering Franchise Operations Manuals in both formats may be an answer that will work for all franchisees!

Chapter 8

OTHER DEVELOPMENT AREAS

Franchise Training Programme

Once a person signs the Franchise Agreement they become a franchisee. However, before they can be permitted to start trading they must have trained in all aspects of the franchise business. It is not sufficient for a franchisee just to have attended the training, what is important is that they have completed their training, and they are of a standard suitable to start operating the franchise.

Most franchisors will include some form of testing and accreditation within the franchise training session and should a franchisee fail to achieve the necessary standard, the franchisor can either require the franchisee attend additional training at the franchisee's cost or the franchise may be revoked.

When developing a franchisee training programme a good starting point is to use the Franchise Operations Manual. As the Franchise Operations Manual contains all the detailed information necessary to run a successful franchise, it makes sense to use it as the basis for franchisee training. In a number of franchise training courses, the franchisor will start on page one of the Franchise Operations Manual and review every page until they get to the end. This way the franchisor knows they have covered everything and also, the franchisee knows that everything is contained with the Franchise Operations Manual, should they need to refer to it in the future.

Other franchisors use the Franchise Operations Manual as a reference document and divide the franchisee training into two distinct parts 1) how to run a franchised business 2) how to sell and deliver the products and services of the franchise.

The how to run a franchised business section of the franchisee's training will cover the standard areas that virtually every business owner needs to know, such as:

- How to form a company
- Data Protection registration
- VAT registration
- Accounting and Bookkeeping
- Insurance
- Health & Safety
- Employing staff

- Training
- Franchisee reporting
- Franchise territories
- National account policies
- Franchisee fee payment process
- Local and national marketing
- IT systems

The how to sell and deliver the products and services of the franchise section of the franchisee's training will cover every aspect relating to the customer and the products and services. If a franchise runs Pre School singing and dance classes, this section would cover in minute detail area such as:

- How to market the classes
- What you do when someone enquiries about a class
- How to book someone on a class
- Taking payment for classes
- How to set-up a class, which may include putting up signage, setting up the room, doing a risk assessment etc.
- How to begin each class which may include taking a register of who attends, how to welcome the children, explaining where the toilets are, telling the adults about the fire exits etc.
- How to run each class which may include what music to play in each session, what equipment to use, how long each section lasts etc.

- How to end a class which may include what to say, telling people when the next class is, what may have to be handed out etc.
- Tidying up after the class which may include how to pack up equipment so that it doesn't get damaged, taking down signage, checking that nothing has been left, telling the venue owner that they are leaving etc.

Clearly the information contained in this section of the Franchisee Training course will differ for each franchise. Training can be done in a classroom format or it may be that training is offsite and undertaken in a real situation through working with someone already doing the role. Whichever approach is taken it is still good practice to keep referring back to the Franchise Operations Manual on the basis that the manual should contain everything the franchisee needs.

The duration of the franchisee training will also vary between franchises. Relatively straightforward franchises may consist of 5 days training in total, undertaken at the franchisors Head Office, with each day run consecutively. Other franchises may require the franchisee to undertaken 4 weeks of training, which is split between Head Office and onsite training, and broken up into week long training sessions with a two week gap between each. The franchising training programme should be as long as is necessary to cover every aspect of the franchised business to ensure that franchisees are competent to start trading at the end of their training.

Franchise Business Plan

The Franchise Business Plan is an essential tool for the franchisee both for raising any funding needed to purchase and operate the franchise, as well as being tool to monitor their progress and keep the business focused on achieving its goals.

Many franchisees will not have created a complete Business Plan before which is why it is common practice for franchisors to provide a Business Plan template. It is important however that franchisees personalise any Business Plan template to reflect the specific conditions in their own franchise territory.

Business Plans should encapsulate long-term targets, estimates and forecasts. Business Plans can be constructed in many ways however one way is shown below:

1. *Summary of your plan*
   Highlighting the attractions of your business
   a) What is the business?
   b) What is the market?
   c) Potential for business.
   d) Forecast profit figures.
   e) How much money is needed?
   f) Prospects for the investor/lender.

2. Franchise background
a) When the franchise started.
b) The number of franchisees within the network.
c) Summary of franchisee past performance.
d) Indication of how relevant or not past franchisee performance is to this franchise.

3. Management
a) The franchisees past employment, skills and relevant experience.
b) List of the key people who will be working in the franchise and their experience.
c) The key franchisor personnel listing their areas of responsibility.

4. The product or service
a) A simple description of what the franchise does.
b) List anything that is unique about the franchised product or service and/or what elements will make it succeed in the face of competition.
c) Competitor analysis.
d) The strategy to win business against the competition.
e) List of Trade Marks and any Patents.

5. Marketing
a) The market:
   - Its size, its past and future growth.
   - Analysis of market into sectors; identify sector your franchise is aimed at.
   - Likely customers: who, type (industrial or consumer), size, how they buy.

- Competitors: who, their size, position in market, likely response to any challenges.
  b) Selling:
  - How to sell (Internet, direct mail, phone, intermediaries, and so on).
  - Who to sell to.
  - What the price will be.

6. Operational details
  a) Where franchisees will be based: the location, type of premises.
  b) What services the franchisor will be providing.
  c) Suppliers.
  d) Equipment needed.

7. Financial analysis
  a) Summary of forecasts.
  b) Monthly profit and loss forecast for five years.
  c) Monthly cash flow forecast for five years.
  d) Forecast balance sheet for five years.
  e) The assumptions behind the forecasts.
  f) The principal risks which could affect projections
  g) SWOT analysis – strengths, weaknesses, opportunities and threats.

8. Prospects
  a) Objectives: short-term and long-term.
  b) The finance needed and what it is needed for.
  c) Shareholdings suggested (if appropriate).

As I stated there are many formats for Business Plans, however the key element is that it must meet the needs of its two main audiences: 1) The banks and other lending organisations 2) The franchisee.

Any lender of finance to the franchisee will want to know whether their funding is safe. A bank will want to know whether the franchisee can afford to pay the interest on any loan and will also want to assess whether they believe the franchise will be a success. An investor will also want to know whether their investment is safe however they will also want to know the likely return on their investment and over what timeframe. Both the banks and investors will want to see a Franchise Business Plan that has been personalised for the franchisees own situation. They will want to see projections based upon the territory the franchisee will be operating in based on what competition already exists. What they don't want to see is

The Franchise Business Plan must meet the needs of the individual franchisee

a standard Business Plan that has been created by the franchisor and the only personalisation has been in changing the franchisees name and contact details. If the Franchise Business Plan does not meet the needs of the banks and investors the franchisee will be unlikely to get the funding they require.

The Franchise Business Plan also has to meet the needs of the individual franchisee. The franchisee amongst other things must be clear about the potential in their territory, what the competition is and the pricing structure required to be successful in their territory. By understanding the market they are going to be operating in and the local influencing factors, the franchisee has the opportunity of running a successful franchised business. Although franchising is about every franchise operating in exactly the same way, there will be different influencing factors on franchisees depending on where they are located, the market potential in their area and who their competitors are. A successful franchisee is one who understands their market and can discuss any local factors that may have an influence on their business with their franchisor.

Franchise Territory Mapping

The majority of franchises operate on an exclusive territory basis. This means that every franchisee will be given a map showing the area in which they will be the only franchisee who will be allowed to market their business in. I specifically wrote "market their business" rather than operate or sell because the law allows customers to choose who they want to do business with. Therefore a customer based in one franchise territory may wish a different franchisee to do business with. What is permissible however is to prevent other franchisees within a network from proactively marketing themselves outside their territory or in the territories of other franchisees. This provides a franchisee with the comfort that they will be able to develop and grow their business, within their territory, without direct competition from other franchisees.

When a franchise model is based on exclusive territories it is important to ensure that the criteria used to define the territories is based upon the key influencing factors for the business. The most common influencing factor is having sufficient potential customers in an area. If you take a lawn care franchise then the criteria used to define a territory should be based on each territory having a minimum number of properties with lawns. It is no good basing a lawn care territory just on population or number of homes, as in one part of a country there may be a higher proportion of homes without gardens such as flats and town houses. If a business is currently successful based on having a certain number of potential customers in your catchment area, then every franchise territory should have the same number of potential customers in their territory, if they are going to replicate the success.

Having defined the franchise territory criteria, a decision will need to be made as to whether to map out the country in advance, predefining each franchise territory or to wait until serious franchisee enquiries are received before mapping out individual territories. The decision is normally down to the number of potential franchise territories available and whether it will be only franchised in specific areas. For some franchises, it may be sensible to split the country into a small number of predefined specific territories. Where a franchise has a large number of potential territories, it makes more sense not to predefine territories.

The problem with predefining territories is that there is likelihood that where a franchisee is based will not be the optimum place to maximise the potential of the territory. If an enquiry is received from any area that borders two or even three predefined territories, it may have a negative impact on their business. Customers may not travel from one side of a territory to the other, preferring to use another company that is closer by. If the franchisee has to deliver products to customers, logistically it is harder and more costly to do if they are based on the edge of their territory rather than being in the centre. Also if two neighbouring franchisees are based very close to each other they may end up competing for business around where they are both based and lose out on business in other parts of their territories.

Therefore when franchising a business, it is a good idea not to predefine the territories. The criteria for territories will still be known and therefore prospective franchisees can be told the criteria so that they understand what the potential is in each franchise territory. However, by not having predefined the territory boundaries it also allows the franchisor to construct a territory for optimum performance dependent on where the franchisee is located. Having a franchisee located in the centre of a territory may be best for the franchisee and their customers, and by not having predefined territories it provides the flexibility for the franchisor to do this.

Another key reason for not predefining territories is that it is important, especially for the first few franchisees in any network, that they are successful, as they will be the bench mark against which other prospective franchisees will view the franchise. If a franchisee underperforms due to their territory not being in the optimum position for them, it will make it much harder to substantiate any franchisee projections that are provides to prospective franchisees. Even if a prospective franchisee does not view this as an issue, they may find that it will be harder to access any funding from a bank or an investor as they are likely to base their lending decision more on how the existing franchisee network is performing rather than the projections of a prospective franchisee.

One of the biggest concerns people have with building territories around franchisees rather than predefining territories, is that the franchisor will be left with areas between existing territories that they cannot sell, because these areas do not meet the minimum criteria required for a territory. This is a valid concern however before making a decision over which approach to take, consideration as to whether it is realistic to expect to be able to sell franchises in absolutely every possible location. For many franchises, selling every conceivable territory is unlikely and it is far better to have franchisees in the territories performing really well, compared with having more franchisees but performing less well.

There is of course a compromise between the two approaches and that is to start by not predefining territories and once a desired number have been sold, to predefine the remaining territories, maximising the potential remaining number of territories that can be sold.

Whichever approach is taken when creating franchise territories the most critically aspect when creating franchise territories is to base the territory on the key influencing factors for the business. Make sure franchisees have the correct potential customer base to generate the level of business required to be successful.

SECTION 3

Franchisee Recruitment

Section Three looks at the whole topic of recruiting franchisees. I will describe the various steps required to successfully recruit franchisees, firstly starting with how to develop a targeted recruitment strategy aimed to create awareness of your franchise opportunity. Once potential franchisees are made aware of your franchise and show interest, I will then cover the various franchise recruitment material that is required throughout the whole recruitment process. I will then look at how to best structure a franchisee interview and finally once a franchisee has signed the Franchise Agreement and become a franchisee, what training they will require and the various ways in which this can be delivered.

This section has been split into five chapters:

Chapter 9 -   Franchise Recruitment Strategy - Part 1
This chapter covers the reasons why every franchisor should have a detailed franchise recruitment strategy, and what the objectives of the strategy should be.

Chapter 10 - Franchise Recruitment Strategy – Part 2
The second chapter covers the various different types of marketing media that can be used to inform people know that franchise opportunities are available.

Chapter 11 - Franchise Recruitment Material

This chapter covers the various pieces of recruitment material that are required, from the initial enquiry form right through to the formal franchise offer letter.

Chapter 12 - Franchise Recruitment

This chapter covers the three elements associated with recruiting franchisees: handling the initial enquiry, interviewing suitable candidates, and finally the process for signing up a franchisee.

Chapter 13 - Franchisee Training

The last chapter in this section covers how to train franchisees. It will discuss the various components that should make up any franchisee training programme and will also look at the various approaches franchisors take in the way they deliver their franchisee training.

Chapter 9

FRANCHISE RECRUITMENT STRATEGY- PART 1

Much of the success of any franchise is down to recruiting the right people as franchisees. With the right people who have both the skills and correct mental attitude required in the franchise, and so long as they are provided with comprehensive training and ongoing support, they will be successful. Conversely, recruiting the wrong people will create far more work for the franchisor, hamper future franchisee recruitment and will ultimately have a negative effect on the profitability for both franchisee and franchisor. Therefore recruiting the right people is essential to the success of the franchise.

Some people ask me why, if franchising is about following a model exactly, it shouldn't make any difference who a franchisor recruits so long as the franchisee does as they are supposed to. My response is that if a franchisor recruits the wrong people as their franchisees, ones who either struggle to learn the franchisors methods or have the wrong attitude and keeps wanting to change the way they run their franchised business, it can cause major problems in the franchise. It is important to accept that not everyone is cut out to be a franchisee. Some people do not enjoy repetitive work for long periods of time, others don't like being told what to do. Unfortunately for these people, being a franchisee is likely to involve both.

Unfortunately many prospective franchisees get caught up in the excitement of owning a business

I have other people who say that surely, if someone is going to buy a franchise then they are not going to buy one if they have issues with they way they will have to work or are not happy following detailed instructions. Unfortunately many prospective franchisees get caught up in the excitement of owning a business and do not fully appreciate or consider what they are letting themselves in for. Given that unhappy or failing franchisees can create a lot of problems for a franchisor it is therefore important that franchisors accept responsibility for only recruiting people that they believe are right as a franchisee.

I regularly explain to franchisors the importance of recruiting the right people as franchisees and every franchisor says they will be very diligent in their franchise recruitment. However, many franchisors get lured into reducing their diligence by prospective franchisees waving cheques! This is partly due to franchisors wanting or needing to recoup the financial outlay they have had in setting up their franchise and partly due to the need to sign up their first franchisees. When I speak to franchisors, in more than 75% of cases, they say they regret at least two or their first four franchisees. They golden rule in franchisee recruitment is to develop a profile of the type of people most suited to being a franchisee of the business and only recruit those people that meet this profile exactly. Do not be tempted to recruit people that only partial meet the franchisee profile under the belief that with extra training and support on your behalf they could become a good franchisee. If a prospective franchisee is not absolutely right do not recruit them.

Franchisee Profile

When developing a profile for your franchisees, some of the most important elements for consideration are:

- The cost of the franchise
- The income that a franchisee is likely to make
- The physical and environmental nature of the franchise
- The time requirements of the franchise
- The role of the franchisee

- Whether franchisees will have to recruit and manage staff
- Any essential skills a franchisee must already have

The total cost of the franchise is likely to dictate the type of people who can afford to buy it. If the total cost of a franchise is £150,000 then not surprisingly the cost is likely to have a bearing on who can buy it. Most banks will lend up to a maximum of 75% of the total cost of a franchise, therefore for a franchise that requires a total investment of £150,000, prospective franchisees will need to have at least £37,500 of their own funds before any borrowing. In addition bank loans over £20,000 are likely to require the franchisee to guarantee the loan, which normally takes the form of a charge on the franchisee's property. If the franchisee does not have they necessary deposit from their own savings or they do not have sufficient assets to secure the loan against then regardless as to whether they have the right skills and attitude to be a successful franchisee they will not be able to afford to buy the franchise in the first place. Therefore when it comes to marketing the franchise, if your franchise has a high cost then only market it in media where the reader is likely to be able to afford it.

Linked to the cost of buying the franchise is the income that the franchise is likely to generate. If a franchise is only going to generate a small income it will have an impact on the type of person who can afford to buy a franchise that will only generate a small income. There is no point franchisors targeting experienced good sales people as their franchisees if the franchise is likely to only earn the franchisee £30,000, good experienced sales people are likely to be earning far more than that already. If a franchise isn't going to generate large income levels for the franchisees perhaps targeting older people as franchisees would be more appropriate. Often, people over 60 years of age have less personal financial commitments and therefore are more prepared to run a business with lower income potential than someone in their early forties who or is more likely to have a family and a mortgage. As with most things, there will always be exceptions however it isn't sensible to base your franchisee recruitment strategy on recruiting people who are exceptions to the norm.

> *The physical and environmental nature of the business will have a direct impact on the type of person who would make a good franchisee*

The physical and environmental nature of your business will have a direct impact on the type of person who would make a good franchisee. A delivery franchise that requires franchisees to load a van and deliver products to customers needs to have franchisees that are physically up to doing the job. A roof tiling franchise needs franchisees that are comfortable working at heights and able to work outside in many types of weather. This may all seem very obvious and hard to believe that anyone would try and buy a franchise that didn't suit them. However I can remember a person applying for a franchise which involved them selling produce on a market stall. When they were asked at the interview whether they had any problems standing at a market stall in all weathers for up to eight hours at a time, the applicant suddenly went very quiet and then explained that they had a bad back which prevented them for standing for any length of time and they had bad circulation. Clearly they were not suitable for working on a market stall for eight hours at a time and in all weathers, however even when the Franchise Prospectus had clearly explained what the franchise involved and the role of the franchisee and the person still applied and attended an interview. When it comes to franchisee recruitment do not assume anything. If something is important then always double check.

There are many different types of franchises. Some are full time franchises requiring franchisees to work weekdays, weekends and evenings. Others can be run as a part-time business, working a few hours a few times a week. If the franchise is a full time business with long hours then franchisees will need a personal life that supports the hours that they will need to work. A person who has to collect young children from school or has a relative to look after is unlikely to be able to dedicate the necessary time to their franchise. However if the franchise is a part-time business that allows the hours to be fitted around other commitments, this may be ideal for this type of person. It is important to find out whether a franchisee has commitments or responsibilities that may have an impact on their time. Given this information franchisor can assess whether the individual's personal situation is suitable for them to be a franchisee.

If the franchise involves franchisees cold calling the public or businesses and selling products direct, many people will be unsuitable. It will not matter how much training is provided, if the franchisee is not able to take the daily rejection associated with cold calling, the franchise is not right for them. If the franchise requires the franchisees to work with numbers, such as a bookkeeping franchise, only take franchisees that are numerate and like figures. If the franchise involves running classes for young children, make sure the franchisee likes and is comfortable with children. It is always possible that a franchisee can run a business where they don't relish the environment they work in or the role they have to undertaken, however unlike a job whereby a person can leave and find another job when they get bored, a franchise is a long term commitment. It is far more likely that a franchisee will make a success and maximise the potential in their territory if they enjoy the role they play and the environment they work in.

Many franchises require the franchisee to employ and manage staff. If this is something franchisees need to do, either from the outset or later on in their franchise, it is important that they can manage staff effectively. Not everyone makes a good manager, regardless of how much training and support they are given. Therefore check prior experience and follow up references. Often people believe they would be a good manager with no real justification. There was a lady who applied to become a franchisee of a contract cleaning company that required her to manage a large team of contract cleaners. When asked about her prior management experience she said that she had never had direct management experience at work but she had managed four builders when she had work done on her kitchen. This is not to say that she might not turn out to be a great manager of people however, the franchisor in question was right to want more evidence that she could manage people before considering selling her the franchise.

There are some franchises that require franchisees to have a certain level of prior experience and skills. A hair dressing franchise that requires franchisees to do hair cutting and styling themselves may require that they have minimum number of years experience in hair dressing. The franchisor may teach the franchisee how to do hair dressing using their systems, processes and approach; however the franchisee will still need a base level of hair dressing skills. A car breakdown franchise may need experienced car mechanics to be their franchisees as the time it would take to train a person with no knowledge would be totally impractical. There are many franchises however that specifically do not want franchisees with any prior technical knowledge preferring to teach franchisees from scratch. So long as the duration of training is not prohibitive, training franchisees with no prior technical knowledge ensures that franchisees operate exactly as the franchisor requires as they have no other knowledge to draw upon.

Having drawn up the ideal franchise profile, it is then possible to develop a marketing strategy that is directed at the right type of people and in the right media.

Recruitment Strategy Objectives

It would be easy to think that the recruitment strategy was purely about marketing the franchise opportunity in a place where potential franchisees might see it. However the franchise recruitment strategy objectives are more complex than that. The recruitment strategy has four key objectives:

1. Generate an awareness of the franchise opportunity
2. Build confidence in the brand
3. Provide comprehensive information to prospective franchisees
4. Operate a recruitment process that identifies suitable franchisees

Creating an awareness of the franchise opportunities is the most obvious objective for a franchisee recruitment strategy. Clearly if no one knows that franchise opportunities are available then no one will enquire. It is important that when people know about the franchise opportunities on offer that they have confidence in the franchise brand. If a business has a bad reputation and their recruitment adverts and recruitment material are poorly written and presented, people will not have the confidence in the brand to follow up on the franchise opportunity.

> *Everywhere a franchise is advertised will say something about the brand and the franchise opportunity*

If Dave's Dodgy Deals is looking to franchise and they advertise their franchise as "we sell anything to anyone in anyway" and their advert shows a picture of a shady character in a long overcoat selling to an old frail woman, most people seeing the advert will not want to be associated with such a brand.

Therefore, everywhere a franchise is advertised will say something about the brand and the franchise opportunity. If it's advertised in the Times or the Economist it will say something different about the brand and the franchise compared with an advert in the Sun or a free paper. A small black and white advert compared to a large full page colour advert will convey a different message. A famous celebrity endorsing a franchise compared with a franchise owner in the advert will again convey a different message about the brand and the franchise. Everywhere and every piece of material used to market the franchise needs to be geared around creating confidence in the brand and the franchise being offered.

The franchise recruitment strategy is also concerned with providing prospective franchisees with all the information they will need to make a valued judgement as to whether the franchise is right for them. Franchise recruitment is not just about selling to anyone willing to buy; otherwise the result is likely to be a network of unsuitable failing franchisees. Franchise recruitment is about finding the right people who can be successful as franchisees. This can only be achieved if people enquiring about a franchise are given all the necessary information to make an informed decision. It is far better to "tell it how it is" rather than embellish or exaggerate the truth. Franchisees that feel the franchisor has misled them will not lead to a good working relationship. Given that contented franchisees are a franchisors best recruitment tool, there is no better way of getting people to buy a franchise than by encouraging them to speak to any franchisee in the network. It is important to start the franchisor/franchisee relationship positively from the outset. Therefore "tell it how it is". If they want to proceed knowing the truth, they are far more likely to be happy as a franchisee than if they feel misled.

The other main objective for the Franchisee Recruitment Strategy is to provide the franchisor with the information needed to make an in depth assessment of a prospective franchisee's suitability. This can only really be achieved by having a standard and objective recruitment process, and ensures that the franchisor receives all the relevant information to make a decision. The Franchise Recruitment Strategy will ensure that systems and processes required to validate the information on prospective franchisees is identified and can be put in place.

Chapter 10

FRANCHISE RECRUITMENT STRATEGY - PART 2

Once a franchise profile has been created, a decision has to be made as to where, when and how the franchise will to be marketed.

I have specifically talked about marketing the franchise opportunity rather than advertising the franchise opportunity since advertising is only one element of the marketing. Marketing is a highly complex topic and there have been thousands of books written on the subject. The Chartered Institute of marketing have defined marketing as "The management process responsible for identifying, anticipating and satisfying customer requirements profitably." There are many different processes that can be used for letting prospective franchisees know of a franchise on offer. As this is a book about franchising and not marketing I will risk the wrath of professional marketers by focussing on just five different marketing approaches that franchisors can include in their Franchise Marketing Plan:

1. Online
2. Off the page
3. Exhibitions, Shows & Events
4. Press Releases
5. Word of Mouth

Online

Online media encompasses both traditionally marketing on the World Wide Web as well as marketing using online Social Media. Taking traditional website marketing first, this can take many forms. The first step when looking at online marketing should be to set up a page on the franchisor's own website, providing details about the franchise offering. Using the franchisor's own website is a free medium and is something most prospective franchisees would look for. I am aware of franchisors that are worried and concerned about promoting their franchise on their own website for fear of how their customers may perceive them, however I struggle to understand the logic of this. Is it plausible to be able to establish a franchise network without customers knowing that the business has franchised? One of the key factors that makes something a franchise rather than another business expansion model is that the franchisee enters a contract with the customer not the franchisor. Customers must be clear who they are contracting with, and it is a legal requirement for franchisees to state on their letterhead, emails and other legal documents that they are a business operated under franchise and independently owned. Therefore customers are inevitably going to release that the company is operating a franchise. The franchisor should either embrace franchising and therefore have no worries about promoting it on their website or not franchise at all.

> *The franchisor should either embrace franchising and therefore have no worries about promoting it on their website or not franchise at all*

Once the franchise offering is published on the franchisor's website there are other websites to consider. These other websites can be split into two categories: 1) franchise websites and 2) non franchise websites.

There are many franchise website directories that franchisors can market their franchise on. The whole nature of the World Wide Web is that any one can register a domain name and anyone can create a website. Typically when people search on the internet they usually scroll down no more than three pages of results and many people will only look on the first page of their search results. Therefore when considering which franchise website to be on, do some simple tests. Type in common words that describe the franchise and see which franchise website directories are on the first page. The franchise needs to be seen by as many people as possible and paying to be on the most popular websites is probably a good starting point. It is essential also to understand, when using any online website directory, what level of enquiry qualification the site undertakes. The franchisor needs to decide whether they want the details of absolutely anyone vaguely interested in the franchise or whether they only want enquiries from people who specifically want the type of franchise on offer and have access to the right level of investment needed for the franchise. A highly qualified approach will reduce the number of enquiries received but it could also mean that those received are likely to be more suitable.

There are a wide range of non franchise specific websites that can be considered. If a franchise is looking for people with specific skills, experience or background then advertising on industry specific websites may be worth considering. A lawn care franchise that only wants experienced golf club green keepers as their franchisees, may decide that standard franchise website directories are less appropriate than being on "Pitchcare", the website for green keepers! For experienced salespeople, advertising the franchise on one of the websites for sales professionals may be appropriate. A part-time franchise targeting mothers with young children as their franchisees may find advertising on a mother and baby or a working mum's website the most effective approach. The benefit with advertising on non franchise websites is that there will not be in as much competition from other franchises compared to if the franchise was advertised on a specialist franchise website directory site. However, if the franchisee profile means that anyone could be a franchisee it may be better to advertise just on franchise website directories, as most people who view these websites are just interested in becoming a franchisee.

Off the Page

Off the page refers to magazine and newspaper advertising. There are a number of magazines dedicated to franchising as well as national and local newspapers that carry regular franchise sections. Historically, off the page advertising was the most popular media for marketing franchise opportunities, however in the last two years off the page advertising has been over taken by online media. The two main issues cited by franchisors as to why they are moving away from off the page advertising is the cost and the lifespan of the advert. Off the page advertising on the whole costs far more than almost all other forms of marketing. In addition, depending on the type of off the page media used an advert may only be current for a month as is the case with most franchise magazines, or a week for most national newspapers. This means that there is only a short time for prospective franchisees to see the advert.

On a positive note however, people that do buy a franchise magazine are usually actively looking for a franchise and therefore a well constructed franchise advert can be very effective. The national and regional newspapers that have a regular franchise section play an important role in making people aware about franchising as an option to owning a business. It is important for franchisors considering advertising using national and regional newspapers to look at the demographics of the readership and compare this against the franchise profile they have created.

Exhibitions, Shows and Events

The UK has a long history of staging regional and national franchise exhibitions and shows. Depending on which franchise exhibition or show a franchise wishes to exhibit at, there will be different entry requirements. A number of the longest running franchise exhibitions require exhibitors to be either members of the British Franchise Association or accredited by the British Franchise Association to "exhibition status". The more recent exhibitions and shows have less stringent exhibitor entry requirements with the exhibition organisers undertaking their own internal review of each franchisor that wishes to exhibit.

Franchise exhibitions and shows run regularly throughout the year

Franchise exhibitions and shows run regularly throughout the year. The largest franchise exhibitions are normally run in February and March and also in October. The smaller franchise exhibitions and shows are then interspersed throughout the remainder of the year.

Franchise exhibitions and shows prove popular with people looking to become franchisees as it gives them an opportunity to see a range of franchises on display at one time, as well as giving people the opportunity to talk to the franchisors. The Franchise exhibitions and shows also have a number of professional franchise service providers who also exhibit. These range from the high street banks that have dedicated franchise departments, to franchise consultants, accountants, solicitors and other franchise media providers. At most franchise shows and exhibitions, seminars are run covering a range of topics for both prospective franchisees and businesses looking to franchise their business.

Not surprisingly, there is a large difference in the cost of exhibiting at a national franchise exhibition compared to a local franchise show. There is also a large difference in the number of people who attend the national franchise exhibitions compared to the local franchise shows. However, local franchise shows should not be discounted as they have the advantage of most visitors to the shows coming from the local area. Therefore if a franchisor is looking to recruit franchisees in a specific part of the country where local franchise shows are run, this can be a good targeted approach to franchise recruitment. The national franchise exhibitions will attract visitors from all over the UK as well as international visitors looking for UK franchise opportunities that would be interested in expanding their franchise operation overseas. Even with the national franchise exhibitions the venue location will have a bearing on the mix of visitors. The two national franchise exhibitions held in London not surprisingly have a greater number of visitors based in London and the South. The one national franchise exhibition held in Birmingham has a greater number of visitors from the Midlands.

In addition to the franchise exhibitions and shows a number of business events include a franchise section. These events range from chamber of commerce events to local business networking events as well as community backed events. As with the local franchise shows these events can be a good way to market a franchise opportunity to a local audience.

Press Releases

Press releases are often a form of marketing that is overlooked by the majority of franchisors. Most media providers, whether they are magazine editors, franchise website directors, or local and national papers, are all looking for interesting stories. The launch of a new franchise often is something of interest to media providers so it is important that a press release is sent to all media editors.

The downside to press releases are that there is no guarantee that it will be published. Media providers do receive more press releases than they have space to publish. This lack of space can also be exacerbated at certain times of the year, such as the lead up to franchise exhibition and shows, as well being affected by other news worthy items. Therefore it is important to think about the timing of when to send your press releases.

Press releases are not only for launching a franchise

There is also a specific format in which media providers will require press releases. The layout, format and information provided is very important if it is going to stand the best chance of getting published. If not experienced in writing press releases, my advice would be to seek the services of a professional press release writer.

Press releases are also not only for when launching a franchise. Anything of news worthy interest should be sent to media providers. This could include a franchisee in the network winning an award, or the fifth, tenth, twenty fifth or fiftieth franchise starting out. The press release could be about a charity event run or attended by a franchisee or it may be about the appointment of new Head Office franchisor staff. The underlining rule with regards press releases is to send regular news worthy press releases that are well written and follow the format expected by the media providers.

When considering who to send press releases to, consider both online and off the page media providers. Also send them to both franchise and non franchise media providers. The press releases should help create awareness of the brand and the franchise opportunities. It should also help build confidence in the franchise as a good and successful franchise. It can also help local franchisees by raising the awareness of the franchisee in their local community which in turn can help their business.

Word of Mouth

Franchisors should not forget to tell people about their franchise. Franchisors and franchisees are likely to come across many people in the daily course of their business. Despite all the money spent on marketing franchises, there will inevitably be people that still don't know about the franchise. Every opportunity should be used to publicise the franchise opportunity. This can be at formal networking events to speaking to local suppliers.

Customers and suppliers can also spread the word about a franchise

Customers and suppliers can also spread the word about a franchise as they will know and come into contact with a far greater number of people than any business on their own. A good way of incentivising franchisees, customers and suppliers to spread the news about franchise opportunities is to operate a Franchise Referral Scheme. This works on the basis that if someone tells someone else about a franchise opportunity and they go on to become a franchisee, the person who originally referred receives a finder's fee. This has the advantage that the finder's fee is only paid out if the person becomes a franchisee. In most cases the person who becomes a franchisee may never have known about the franchise opportunity without being informed by the referrer. Even when the franchisee did know about the franchise opportunity, the additional mention of it by a referrer may be the final point that gets them to make contact.

There are two golden rules when it comes to running a Franchise Referral Scheme:

1. Make sure the financial reward is sufficient enough. If only offering a small reward, most people will not put themselves out to spread the word.

2. Make sure the referrer is paid when a franchisee signs up. This may sound obvious but I know of many occasions where the franchisor does not

pay the finders fee. The franchisor tries to get out of paying either by trying to say that the franchisee had already made contact with the franchisor first or they just hope the referrer will forget. Nothing is likely to stop future referrals more, than a franchisor that doesn't pay out when they should. It can also give the franchisor a bad name, damaging the franchisors brand.

Other Marketing Mediums

There are of course many other marketing methods that I have not mentioned, such as: direct mail campaign, in store posters and shop windows advertisements, in street signage such as bill boards and telephone kiosks, train station signs, and specific sector media such as armed forces media, ethnic minority media, gay media, and specialist media targeting the over 50's.

Social media is an area which is growing at an expediential rate

Social Media is an area which is growing at an expediential rate. Many franchisors are using various social media platforms such as LinkedIn, facebook, You Tube and twitter to spread the word about their franchise opportunities. Unlike other marketing media, Social Media is creating its own rules. Social Media is more about giving help and advice and in return people viewing personal and business profiles in a positive light. For instance a franchisor could reply to a Social Media posting from someone asking about what to look for in a franchise and provide them with a set of questions they could ask a franchisor. There is no need to mention specifically that they have franchise opportunities themselves, however if the franchisor has been helpful the person who posted the question may well visit the franchisor's website and find their franchise opportunity. I am sure that by the time you read this book, there will be new Social Media platforms and sites with new protocols for their use. The important thing to remember is that if the type of person who fits the franchisee profile is someone who uses Social Media then choosing not to use social media to market the franchise will be at the franchisor's peril!

Franchise Recruitment Material

I will only touch on this topic here as later I will be covering the different pieces of franchise recruitment material required in more depth. This section is to clarify what the objectives of the Franchise Recruitment Strategy are and how these need to be reflected in the Franchise Recruitment Material used.

The Franchise Recruitment Strategy has four key objectives:

1. Generate an awareness of the franchise opportunity
2. Build confidence in the brand

3. Provide comprehensive information to prospective franchisees
4. Operate a recruitment process that identifies suitable franchisees

This means that all online listing and adverts, off the page adverts, exhibition and show displays, press releases, and word of mouth campaigns need to convey these four objectives.

Depending on the media used there may be additional information to convey such as: no prior experience is required, what the cost of the franchise is, the earning potential, the level of training and support provided, the existence of successful franchisee network, or it may be that the high street franchise banks have already prior approved the franchise for franchisee funding. Every franchise will have different messages that it wishes to convey. The risk is trying to convey too much information in too small a space or time. The key objective of the franchise recruitment material is to provide sufficient information to allow the right people to progress to the next stage of the franchise recruitment process.

Franchise Recruitment Plan

When developing any strategy whether it is how to recruit franchisees or how to launch a new product or service, it is important to formalise it by writing it down. Having created a clear franchisee profile and identified the various media that your franchisee profile person sees and hears, it is time to create your franchise recruitment plan.

The Franchise Recruitment Plan should be a twelve month plan showing what media will be used and when to market the franchise opportunity. This is where budgets come into play. There are lots of different media that could be used to market a franchise, some of which are likely to be prohibitively expensive. I am sure most franchisors would love to run a TV based franchise recruitment campaign however it is far too costly. What is important though, is to have sufficient budget allocated to marketing the franchise opportunity. I have seen many businesses that have spent lots of money creating their Franchise Development Model and then investing on their Infrastructure Development only to be left very little money to let people know that they have franchise opportunities. As with any other part of a business, if a business doesn't let their customers know that they have something for sale then very few people will ever buy it, and this is no different for franchisee recruitment. Before even starting down the road of franchising it is important to have a clear plan of how much franchising is going to cost,

> *The Franchise Recruitment Plan should be a twelve month showing what media will be used and when*

including franchise recruitment marketing. If the necessary funds are not available do not start down the franchising route, as it is far better to wait until they are and then do it properly.

When creating the Franchise Recruitment Plan it is a good idea to use a mix of different marketing media in order to give the best chance for the franchise opportunity to be seen by all those people that fit the franchisee profile. It is usual for franchisors to use all five different marketing media, discussed earlier in this chapter, rather than to stick to just one medium. With online media, consider which franchise and non franchise websites are the most likely ones that a person who meets the franchise profile will visit. Are there certain Social Media platforms that would be appropriate to use? Will there be a franchise page on the franchisor's website? Investigate which off the page publications are the best to advertise in and which are within the overall marketing budget. Are there national or local franchise exhibitions, shows and events that would be good to have a presence at? Could a series of press releases be produced to publicise the launch of the franchise and then other news worthy items throughout the year? Could others spread the word about the franchise opportunities and is there going to be a Franchise Referrer's Scheme?

Having drawn up a list of all the ways to market the franchise opportunity, plan how often to action each media activity and what the associated costs will be. There are often ways to keep marketing costs down whilst having a presence on many marketing mediums. Companies that produce off the page franchise magazines often also have online franchise website directories they will give free entry on so long as advertising is taken in their magazine. Many exhibition organisers will give exhibitors a free entry in their franchise show guide and on their website.

There are also certain times of the year that may be better to market in certain media. If considering advertising in one of the national newspapers it may be better to advertise when there are other high profile franchise events happening such as a national franchise exhibition or national franchise awards, and benefit from the increased coverage of franchising the paper gives that week. Certain national newspapers have a weekly franchise calendar whereby each week they focus on a specific industry sector. Therefore a hair dressing franchise may wish to advertise in the week when the national newspaper is focussing on hair dressing rather than the week they are focusing on pet franchises.

Having worked out what media to market in, when, the frequency to do it, and the cost, it is time to create the twelve month Franchise Recruitment Plan. There are many project management software programmes or spreadsheets available, however whatever is used the most important point is to create a hard copy of the plan. Make sure the Franchise Recruitment Plan is split into weeks of the year and mark on it when each activity is going to take place as this allows an easy visual graphic representation of the Franchisee Recruitment Plan. It will also highlight gaps in the year when not enough marketing is happening or when there is too much marketing occurring.

Evaluation

Evaluating the success of each marketing activity undertaken is an area that is often overlooked. Despite all the franchise profiling and optimising the type, frequency and timing of the marketing, there will always be some marketing activities that prove less successful than others. It is important therefore that systems and processes are in place to be able to know which activities are working better than others.

A simple way of recording which activities are producing the best results is to ask every person that enquires about the franchise where they heard about it from. Some enquiries will be obvious such as "filled out a form" on a franchise exhibition stand. Others may be leads that come directly from a franchise website directory, others may be from someone who emails or phones direct. Ask where they heard about the franchise; did they see an advert in the national newspaper, a magazine or a press release they

> *Evaluating the success of each marketing activity undertaken is an area that is often overlooked*

read? Sometimes it may be that the franchise opportunity was seen in a number of places before going on to the franchisor's website to register their interest. Ensure that a record is kept of everywhere that a franchise is seen. This will allow the franchisor to stop marketing in media not producing results and redirect their expenditure either to increase marketing in the places that are working or to try other previously untried media.

When evaluating the success of marketing media it is important to give the medium sufficient time to be able to properly evaluate its success. When advertising in a national newspaper it is best to advertise in at least two issues before being in a position to properly evaluate its success. For franchise exhibitions evaluating success is unlikely to be any earlier than six months after the event as many people take a long time to decide the franchise of their choice. With online franchise directory websites it would be more appropriate to evaluate the success after three months. It is also important to mark on the Franchise Recruitment Plan against each marketing activity when evaluation will take place, as this ensures the best use of the franchisors recruitment marketing budget.

Chapter 11

FRANCHISE RECRUITMENT MATERIAL

Having developed the Franchise Recruitment Strategy the next step is to create all the forms, documents and letters required to start to process enquiries for the franchise. These forms, documents and letters are then combined together to form the Franchise Recruitment Pack.

The Franchise Recruitment Pack should contain everything required to handle an initial enquiry right through to signing up a franchisee. Typically, a Franchise Recruitment Pack will contain fifteen to twenty different pieces of recruitment material and can include amongst others:

1. Franchise Recruitment Process Map
2. Franchise Enquiry Form
3. Franchise Brochure

4. Franchise Brochure Letter

5. Franchise Application Form

6. Franchise Application Form Letter

7. Invitation to a Franchise Interview Letter

8. Decline for a Franchise Interview Letter

9. Confirmation of a Franchise Interview Letter

10. Confidentiality Agreement

11. Franchise Disclosure Pack

12. Provisional Franchise Offer Letter

13. Franchise Rejection Letter

14. Deposit Agreement

15. Deposit Agreement Letter

16. Franchise Agreement

17. Franchise Agreement Letter

18. Reference Request Letter

19. Formal Franchise Offer Letter

20. Franchise Training Confirmation Letter

Franchise Recruitment Process Map

The Franchise Process Map is a flow chart showing each step of the recruitment process, referencing each document that is required, and contained within the Franchise Recruitment Pack.

The first stage of the Franchise Recruitment Process Map should deal with what happens when an enquiry is received about the franchise. The Franchise Recruitment Process Map will show what to do. It will say what to do to follow up on the enquiry, what happens when the enquirer wants to progress with their franchise application, at what stage to interview an applicant, what legal documents the applicant signs and when, and the process the applicant goes through when signing the franchise agreement.

The Franchise Process Map is a flow chart showing each step of the recruitment process

There are many steps in the Franchise Process Recruitment Map that have a number of options, such as continue to process the enquiry, decide not to take the application any further, or required additional information before proceeding. At each step, the Franchise Recruitment Process Map should state the relevant course of action, whether any document or form is required, and if so where in the franchise recruitment pack the document or form can be found.

By following a systemised process for franchisee recruitment, it will ensure that all franchisees receives the relevant information, at the right time, needed to make a valued judgement as to whether the franchise is right for them. It will also ensure that the franchisor receives all the necessary information to decide whether an applicant is right for their franchise.

Franchise Enquiry Form

The Franchise Enquiry Form is usually placed on the franchisor's website allowing people interested in the franchise to complete basic information themselves. The franchisor can then send out details about the franchise opportunity. The objective of the franchise enquiry form is not to qualify prospective applicants rather to enable the franchisor to start a dialogue with interested people.

Typically the enquiry form will ask for:

- Name
- Contact address
- Contact telephone number(s)
- Email address

Often the enquiry form will also ask:

- What area of the country the applicant is looking for a franchise in
- The timescale when they would be looking to become a franchisee

- Where the applicant heard about the franchise, so that you can evaluate the success of your marketing strategy.

The final elements contained on an enquiry form are:

- An explanation of what will happen with their enquiry such as a Franchise Brochure will be emailed or posted to the applicant and the franchisor will contact the applicant within 5 days
- A privacy statement saying that the applicants contact details will not be shared with anyone else without the applicant's prior agreement.

The enquiry form is the start of the Franchisee Recruitment Process and it is important not to discourage any prospective franchisee at this stage. I have seen enquiry forms that are five pages long and ask for a huge amount of information before sending the applicant any information. This is likely to deter applicants especially because at this initial stage the applicant probably has no real idea as to whether the franchise would be right for them, and they just want to find out basic information.

Remember that this may well be the first point of contact that a franchisor has with a prospective franchisee, so first impressions count. If too much information is asked for, or the franchisor's questions are perceived to be unreasonable or unnecessary at this first stage of registering an interest in a franchise, there is a real risk that the interested person will be put off completing it and look elsewhere for a franchise.

Franchise Brochure

The Franchise Brochure, also referred to as the Franchise Prospectus, is primarily a high level summary of the franchise. The information contained within the Franchise Brochure should not be confidential and it is in my view, just as much about weeding out those people for whom the franchise is totally unsuitable for, as it is about trying to promote the franchise. Usually Franchise Brochures are constructed to convey the following information:

- What is the franchise about and what would a franchisee do?
- How much does the franchise cost and what would someone get for their money?
- How much would a franchisee be likely to earn?
- The type of person most suited to be a franchisee, in other words a summary of the franchisee profile
- Answers to frequently asked questions such as: is finance available, how long is the training, what ongoing fees does a franchisee pay, are the franchisee earnings guaranteed?

By providing this information, it should deter those people who: don't want to do the role a franchisee will be required to undertake, find the franchise is too expensive, the earning potential is not sufficient for them and those that don't meet the requirements needed to be a franchisee.

Those people that read the Franchise Brochure and feel that the franchise may be right for them and meet the requirements as a franchisee, and have prequalified themselves, the franchisor knows that they are serious about the franchise.

The Franchise Brochure is likely to be the first piece of franchise recruitment material that a prospective franchisee will receive. It is therefore critical that the format, style and design of the brochure conveys all the information and messages that prospective franchisees need to know in respect of both the franchise and the franchisors brand. If the franchise cost is high and is targeted at selling luxury products and services, it is not a good idea to have a Franchise Brochure in black and white,

The Franchise Brochure is likely to be the first piece of franchise recruitment material that a prospective franchisee will receive

without any graphics and printed on poor quality paper. Look to produce a glossy expensive looking Franchise Brochure that reflects the products and services sold. It is for this reason that a Rolls Royce car brochure is far more expensive looking than a Ford car brochure. The brochure needs to reflect the type of business you are in.

There is always a debate about whether the Franchise Brochure should be in a printed or electronic format. There are arguments made for both cases. An electronic brochure is easier to send and allows a quicker response to an enquiry. The downside is that if the person to whom it is sent prints it off and they do not have a good quality printer, the printed end result may not be of a standard that reflects the type and quality of the franchise business. Many people say that the recipient may only view it onscreen or will accept that the poor quality is down to them and nothing to do with the franchisor. Other franchisors prefer posting a printed copy of the franchise brochure as they can control the quality of what the person receives. It also enables them to send examples of their products if they so wish. I know a franchisor which sells luxury jams and chutneys and sends a sample pack of their leading selling products along with the franchise brochure. They believe that it will allow the person who enquires to try the product and are confident that it will put the franchisor in a good light.

The downside to posting printed versions of the Franchise Brochure is the cost and the time it takes. Ultimately the decision to produce a hard copy Franchise Brochure that is posted or an electronic version that is emailed or downloadable from the franchisor's website is something that each franchisor needs to decide for themselves.

Franchise Brochure Letter

Regardless as to whether posting or emailing the Franchise Brochure, the Franchise Brochure will need to be accompanied by either a letter or an email, thanking the person for their enquiry and explaining what they need to do if having read the franchise brochure they want to continue with their application.

This Franchise Brochure Letter or Email does not need to be complex however it is important that it supports the messages being conveyed in the Franchise Brochure. Rather than making up a different letter or email each time, it makes more sense to construct a letter or email that can be used with the majority of Franchise Brochures sent. The only time to vary the letter or email would be to answer a specific question raised by the person enquiring, or where the information provided on the enquiry form requires a specific response such as the area they are enquiring about has already been taken but a nearby territory is available.

Franchise Application Form

For those that request a Franchise Brochure and on receiving it wishes to continue with their application, the next step in the recruitment process should be to collect information on the applicant. This will allow the franchisor to decide whether the applicant meets their franchisee profile and it is worth the franchisor continuing with the application.

Having a standard Franchise Application Form will ensure that the appropriate information is collected on each applicant to allow the franchisor to asses the applicant's suitability. Typically a Franchise Application Form will be made up of seven sections:

1. Detailed personal information about the applicant such as address, if they have a spouse or partner, children or dependents.
2. Educational background and qualifications.
3. Employment history which should show who they worked for and what roles they had in each job, and for how long.
4. Financial standing should indicate whether they would need to borrow to finance their franchise or they have the financial resources already, details of their bank for future references, and whether they have ever been declared a bankrupt.
5. Details of at least two people who will act as personal references.
6. Answers to questions about their suitability to be a franchisee and to carry out the franchisee role.
7. An opportunity for the applicant to provide any other relevant information that they would like the franchisor to consider.

The Franchise Application Form can either be in a printed version or in an electronic format. As the Franchise Application Form is a factual document rather than a promotional document there is less of a need for franchisors to spend money on graphic design, although any form or document that an applicant receives will reflect on the applicant's perception of the franchisor.

Franchise Application Form Letter

When the Franchise Application Form is sent, it will need to be either posted or emailed with instructions on how the applicant should complete it and what they need to do with it once completed. As with the franchise brochure letter, the accompanying franchise application form letter or email does not need to be complex. It just needs to provide the applicant with clear instructions as to what to do and what will happen with the Franchise Application Form once received.

It is important for franchisors to always follow through with any statements of intent

The Franchise Application Form process should be the same for all applicants. Therefore it should be possible to create a Franchise Application Form Letter or Email that can be used when sending all Franchise Application Forms. A standard letter or email will prevent the franchisor from having to construct a new letter or email each time saving time and ensuring a consistent message is conveyed.

It is important for franchisors to always follow through with any statements of intent mentioned in the Franchise Application Form Letter. If it says that the franchisor will reply to the applicant within fourteen days, the franchisor must ensure that the do. Better still, the franchisor should respond before fourteen days as this will say to the applicant that the franchisor exceeds expectations and delivers on what they say.

Invitation to a Franchise Interview Letter

On receipt of a completed Franchise Application Form, the franchisor will need to make a judgement as to whether the applicant meets the franchise profile. If following review of the Franchise Application Form they believe the applicant may be suitable as a franchisee, they will need to invite the applicant to an interview. The interview will be the first opportunity for the applicant to find out more information about the franchise so that they can make a valued judgement as to whether they franchise will be right for them. The interview will also allow the franchisor the opportunity to find out more about the applicant and assess further their suitability as a franchisee.

The Franchise Interview Letter will explain that following a review of their completed Franchise Application Form that the applicant may have the qualities required to become a franchisee and they are invited to an interview. The Franchise Interview Letter should explain what format the interview will take, where it will be held and how long it will last. Finally it should ask the applicant to make contact with the franchisor to arrange a date for the interview.

Decline for a Franchise Interview Letter

If on receipt of the completed application form the applicant clearly doesn't meet the profile then the franchisor should reject the application and not be tempted to pursue the application on the off chance that the applicant may be suitable with additional training or support. The franchisor has a moral and legal responsibility of protecting the financial investment of not just the individual franchisee but all the franchisees in their network, and a failing franchisee can damage a franchise brand not just for the franchisor but for all franchisees.

If the franchisor does not wish to take an application any further it is important to inform the applicant of the decision. It is usually best in these situations to keep the decline letter brief and to the point. Do not be tempted to try and give detailed reasons for the decision as it can give an applicant a reason to try and object. It is better to say that recruiting the right people for the franchise who have the best chance to succeed as a franchisee is essential to the success of the business and the whole franchisee network and that after reviewing the applicant's information that it was decided that they did not meet the specific franchisee criteria.

Confirmation of a Franchise Interview Letter

Once a date for the franchise interview has been arranged it is good practice for the franchisor to write to the applicant and confirm the details for the interview. This ensures that there is no confusion regarding the format or purpose of the interview.

The Franchise Interview Letter will also usually have a Confidentiality Agreement attached to it. The Franchise Interview Letter should explain that at the interview the franchisor will need to provide the applicant with confidential information so that they can make an informed decision about the franchise opportunity. As this information is confidential the franchisor will ask that the applicant signs the Confidential Agreement and returns it to them in advance of the meeting.

Confidentiality Agreement

The Confidentiality Agreement is a legal document and therefore should be produced by a suitably qualified person. The Confidentiality Agreement should state that the information that the applicant is provided with needs to be kept confidential and can only be used by the applicant to assess whether or not to become a franchisee. The information is not allowed to be shown or discussed with anyone that has not signed a confidentiality agreement. It will also state that should the franchisor request, the applicant must destroy all confidential information and confirm in writing that this has been done.

Prospective franchisees should not have any issue with signing a Confidentiality Agreement as it shows that the franchisor is taking the necessary precautions to protect the confidential information about the franchise which should it become public knowledge could damage the franchise brand and affect the business of their franchisees.

Prospective franchisees should not have any issue with signing a Confidentiality Agreement

Despite asking for a signed copy of the Confidentiality Agreement to be sent to the franchisor before the interview, it is not uncommon for applicants to forget to do so! It is therefore important that the franchisor has a copy of the Confidentiality Agreement to hand when the applicant turns up for their interview. The applicant can then sign the Confidentiality Agreement there and then. If they are not prepared to sign the Confidentiality Agreement, it is important that the interview does not take place.

Franchise Disclosure Pack

At the franchise interview, the applicant will need to be informed of everything about the franchise opportunity in order to assess whether the franchise is right for them. In order to ensure that all relevant information is given to an applicant it is usual to provide the applicant with a Franchise Disclosure Pack. In some countries where there is specific legislation that dictates what information must be provided to an applicant and in what format, in the UK there is no such

A franchisor should not withhold any pertinent information

requirement. However just because there is no legislation in the UK stating what information must be provided to a prospective franchisee, it does not mean that a franchisor should withhold any pertinent information.

Consequently Franchise Disclosure Packs vary greatly in their structure. To provide prospective franchisees with all the necessary information they will require, a typical structure for a Franchise Disclosure Pack would be:

1. Background on the franchisor business.
2. An assessment of the market for the franchisors products and services.
3. Details relating to the Franchise Package such as; what it costs and what a franchisee gets for their money.
4. Details relating to terms of the franchise such as how long the franchise is for, what happens if a franchisee wants to renew, the ongoing fees a franchisee will pay, the legal status that a franchisee must operate under. In addition it needs to provide details on whether the franchisee will operate from home or commercial premises, whether a franchisee has to register for VAT before commencing their business, the policy regarding national accounts and many important terms relating to the franchise.
5. The Franchise territory criteria and whether franchises will be offered on an exclusive or non exclusive basis and what this means in practice to the franchisee.

6. Any minimum performance requirements that the franchisee must meet such as minimum income levels, minimum local marketing spend, or any other minimum performance criteria relevant to the franchise.
7. The obligations that the franchisee must meet.
8. The obligations that the franchisor must meet.
9. The franchisee profile.
10. A SWOT analysis explaining what the Strengths, Weaknesses, Opportunities and Threats are to the franchise.
11. Detailed franchisee financial projections.

The Franchise Disclosure Pack is given to the applicant at the interview and they should be permitted to write on it and take it away with them. Therefore it is essential that the applicant has signed the Confidentiality Agreement before being given the franchise disclosure document.

Provisional Franchise Offer Letter

If following the franchise interview the franchisor believes that the applicant is suitable to be a franchisee many franchisors will offer the applicant a provisional franchise, subject to suitable references being received and the applicant being happy to sign the Franchise Agreement.

It is not uncommon for franchisors to place a time limit on the provisional offer. Where a time limit is imposed, it is important that the time limit is realistic and allows the prospective franchisee sufficient time to take legal advice regarding the Franchise Agreement and to put in place any funding requirements they should need. A reasonable time limit for a provisional franchise offer is one calendar month.

Do not put undue time pressure on prospective franchisees

Whilst the prospective franchisee is making their final decision as to whether to accept the franchise offer it is usual that the franchisor agrees not to pursue any further enquiries regarding the franchise territory in question. The British Franchise Association has a ruling that they do not want franchisors to put undue time pressure on prospective franchisees by operating a time is of an essence policy whereby the first person to come up with the money gets the franchise.

If a franchisor makes the decision not to pursue any further enquiries regarding the franchise territory then the franchisee needs to demonstrate some form of commitment of their intention to become a franchisee subject to the franchise agreement being acceptable and funding being available. Therefore franchisors often ask that prospective franchisee pay a deposit whilst the prospective franchisee makes a final decision.

The Provisional Franchise Offer Letter needs to state that the franchisor is making a provisional offer relating to a specific franchise territory. It also needs to state what the conditions of the provisional offer are and what the applicant needs to do to accept the provisional offer.

Franchise Rejection Letter

If following the franchise interview the franchisor decides that the applicant is not suitable to be a franchisee, they need to write and inform the person of their decision.

As with the Decline for Interview Letter, it is usual to keep a Franchise Rejection Letter brief and to the point. Therefore a brief letter thanking them for attending the interview but informing them that they have been unsuccessful in the application and wishing them every success in finding a suitable franchise can suffice.

Deposit Agreement

As with the Confidentiality Agreement, the Deposit Agreement is a legal document and therefore should be produced by a suitably qualified individual. The Deposit Agreement will acknowledge that the deposit has been paid and specify the territory that the deposit relates to. It also outlines the conditions under which the deposit agreement is paid. These conditions are that the deposit is refundable less any direct costs incurred by the franchisor should the applicant or the franchisor decide not to go through with the franchise. It will also state the time limit that the deposit relates to and what happens after, should the time limit be reached. Finally it will state that should the applicant decide to go ahead with the franchise that the

It outlines the conditions under which the deposit agreement is paid

money paid as the deposit will be credited against the initial franchise fee payable when the Franchise Agreement is signed.

It is important that the applicant signs and dates the Deposit Agreement and returns it to the franchisor for their records.

Deposit Agreement Letter

The Deposit Agreement Letter accompanies the Deposit Agreement and explains what the applicant should do with the Deposit Agreement should they wish to accept the provisional offer.

It is also normal for the Deposit Agreement Letter to highlight the key conditions under which the deposit is made, as well as stating how and in what format the deposit funds should be paid.

Franchise Agreement

The Franchise Agreement is the contractual agreement between the franchisor and franchisee. Once the Deposit Agreement has been signed and the deposit paid, then the franchisor will send the applicant the Franchise Agreement. It is worth stating that some franchisors do away with any deposit or deposit agreement and just send applicants that they feel are suitable as franchisees, the Franchise Agreement.

The Franchise Agreement should not be a discussion document

The contents of the Franchise Agreement have already been covered in detail earlier in this book, and therefore there is no need to repeat the same material. However, what is worth stressing is that the Franchise Agreement should not be a discussion document. It is important that all franchisees, wherever possible sign up to the same Franchise Agreement. This ensures consistency across the franchise network and reduces any potential for complaints from franchisees comparing the terms of their Franchise Agreements, and makes it easier for the franchisor to monitor and enforce compliance across the whole network.

The main reason for sending a prospective franchisee the Franchise Agreement and recommending they take legal advice over its contents is to ensure that they are fully aware of what they will be signing and their legal obligations. If in exceptional circumstances a change is required to the Franchise Agreement for a specific franchisee, this should be done in the form of a side letter attached to the standard franchise agreement stating what clause has been changed and to what.

Franchise Agreement Letter

The Franchise Agreement Letter accompanies the Franchise Agreement and explains what the prospective franchisee should do with the agreement. It should advise them to seek legal advice from a specialist franchise solicitor to ensure they understand what they are signing and their obligations.

The Franchise Agreement Letter will explain what the prospective franchisee should do if they wish clarification of any point contained within the Franchise Agreement and what they should do if they wish to accept the terms of the Franchise Agreement and become a franchisee.

The Franchise Agreement Letter should also state that the franchise offer is conditional upon the franchisor receiving suitable references on the prospective franchisee and asking for their written confirmation to contact the people listed as referees in the original Franchise Application Form.

Reference Request Letter

Although many franchisors decide not to take personal references on their prospective franchisees I believe that it is a step in the recruitment process that should not be missed out.

Personal references are the last check that a franchisor has before they allow a prospective franchisee to sign the Franchise Agreement. If a reference comes back as unsatisfactory or the applicant refuses to allow the franchisor to contact the named referees, this may be reason for the franchisor to take additional steps to verify the prospective franchisee's suitability.

Personal references are the last check that a franchisor has

The Personal Reference Letter should be sent to the people listed as referees on the Franchise Application Form, and should state that the franchisor is considering offering the applicant a franchise. It should explain the role the franchisee will be required to undertake and ask the referees to confirm the involvement they have had with the applicant and their own personal assessment of the applicant's suitability for the role of a franchisee.

Formal Franchise Offer Letter

If the applicant's references are in order, the franchisor will send a formal offer letter. This Formal Franchise Offer Letter will stipulate who the offer is made to and the territory in question. It will also explain the process that the applicant must follow to accept the offer, which is usually to sign the Franchise Agreement and pay the Initial Franchise Fee less any deposit payment that have already been made.

Franchise Training Confirmation Letter

This is the final document in the Franchise Recruitment Pack. The Franchise Training Confirmation Letter confirms to the applicant that they are now a franchisee. It also states the date, time, duration and venue of the franchisee training and any preparation they should do before the franchisee attends their franchisee training.

Franchise Recruitment Pack Summary

The Franchise Recruitment Pack is an essential compilation of all the documents required in the franchise recruitment process. Constructed properly the Franchise Recruitment Pack will provided a step by step guide to recruiting franchisees and will ensure that the same process is followed for every applicant.

Chapter 12

FRANCHISEE RECRUITMENT

Initial Enquiry Handling

Having spent so much time and money developing the franchise development model, undertaking all the infrastructure development, creating and implementing the franchise recruitment strategy, it amazes me how poorly many franchisors handle the franchise enquiries they get.

One would imagine that everything would be geared towards getting enquiries and once received everything possible done to recruit the right people as franchises. However, for some reason many franchisors do not create a plan for how they are going to effectively handle franchise enquiries when they receive them.

There are four questions to ask when developing the Initial Franchise Enquiry plan: Why, What, When and Who.

Why?

This may seem obvious but any plan should always start by stating what the objective is. So it is important to ask yourself <u>why</u> you are developing an Enquiry Handling Plan. For most franchisors, the objective of the franchise enquiry plan will be to:

- To recruit a specific number of people that are suitable to be franchisees
- To portray a professional image to everyone that enquires about the franchise

Some franchisors want to recruit as many suitable franchisees as possible, however it is important to question whether there is a limit on the number of franchisees that can be recruited, trained and effectively set-up in business in any one year. There may be a limit due to the nature of the franchise, such as acquiring and fitting out suitable premises. Other franchisors may want to limit the number of franchisees they recruit as they only want to recruit, in the first instance, franchisees that will be based close to the franchisor in order to develop the franchisors brand in a specific part of the country before expanding nationwide. It may also be that

Is there a limit on the number of franchisees that can be recruited, trained and effectively set-up in business in any one year?

the level of internal resources required to effectively set-up and support a franchisee limits the number of franchisees that a franchisor can effective recruit. Franchisors need to be clear how many franchisees they want to recruit and make this part of their written enquiry handling objective.

The other main factor to consider for enquiry handling is that regardless as to whether the person who enquires goes on to become a franchisee or not, the manner in which the enquiry is handled will leave a lasting impression with the individual. The person who enquires may be a future potential customer for the franchisor or one of their franchisees. If they have a bad experience with the way their franchise enquiry was handled, they may be left with a negative impression of the whole franchise brand. This could result in them choosing not to purchase the franchise, and telling others of their bad experience. It is therefore important that every person who enquires, regardless as to whether they go on to become a franchisee or not, leaves with a positive impression of the brand.

What?

It is important to have specific and clear enquiry handling objectives with regards to what type of communication process will be used for franchise enquiries.

Decide on the best process to ensure that potentially suitable people, who enquire about the franchises, are not lost due to the way their enquiry is handled. The answer may be to ensure that 100% of people who enquire are sent an acknowledgment, followed by a Franchise Brochure with a covering letter, followed by a personal phone call.

Ensure that everyone will have a good perception of the franchise. It is important that every piece of information and/or correspondence a person receive is of a standard that the business wants to be associated with. This is why it is important to create the Franchise Recruitment Pack, containing every piece of recruitment material that will be required. This will prevent emails and letters being sent out with typing mistakes or pieces of information missing.

It is also important to respond to any questions that are made in the enquiry. Often enquiry forms contain a section where a person can ask specific questions. If someone does ask specific questions ensure that when the Franchise Brochure and covering letter are sent out, that all questions raised are answered. Most people find it very frustrating to ask questions only to be sent a standard reply which either does not address their question at all or only glosses over it. Create the right impression by making sure time is taken to fully answer any question asked.

When?

Timing is critical when dealing with franchisee enquiries. The speed an enquiry is acknowledged will say a lot about the franchise. If they receive an acknowledgment within 30 minutes of making the enquiry, it will give the impression of an efficient business. What if they only receive an acknowledgment the following day? It may be that both timescales would be acceptable, however if you are in potential competition with other franchises, ensure everything is done to handle the enquiry better than the competition. With today's technology it is easy to set-up an automated system that replies to an enquiry as it is received.

Decide when to send the Franchise Brochure and the covering letter/email. The fact that someone has enquired about the franchise probably means they have spent time also looking at a range of franchises. If emailing the Franchise Brochure, it will create a better impression if the person receives it the same day rather than days later. If posting the Franchise Brochure, make sure the person receives it the following day. The cost of posting the Franchise Brochure guaranteed next day delivery compared with second class is relatively small however the impression it will leave with the person who enquires will be very positive.

The timing of the follow up needs careful consideration

The timing of the follow up also needs careful consideration, as there is a fine line between being viewed as too eager, putting the person under pressure and taking too long and being viewed as disinterested. It is important to state in the Franchise Brochure Covering Letter when they will be contacted to discuss the franchise opportunity and answer any questions they may have. It is reasonable to allow a person two or three days to digest what they have been sent before contacting them. Whatever timescales are decided on for each step in the enquiry handling process, it is essential to keep to them.

Who?

Understanding what needs to take place is only part of the Initial Enquiry Handling plan. A decision is needed as to who is going to do each task. A number of franchisors outsource their franchise enquiry handling. Others allocate the tasks to junior members of staff, where as others give the job to senior members of staff or the owners of the business.

Often the reasons why franchisors outsource their enquiry handling is two fold: 1) they do not believe they have the time to handle the enquiries 2) they believe that an outsourced company will handle them better than they can.

As a general rule, I am not a fan of outsourcing enquiry handling. When a person enquires about a franchise, they want to have their enquiry acknowledged, and be forwarded suitable information about the franchise opportunity. Perhaps an outsourced company has the resources to handle the enquiries in a more timely and efficient way than the franchisor, but the area that most outsourced enquiry handling companies struggle with is in answering specific questions that may be asked. They also normally lack the passion and enthusiasm about the franchise that a member of staff or the owners of the business can convey.

The way the enquiry is handled is likely to be the first real impression a prospective franchisee will get of the brand. If the impression required is one of an efficient but impersonal company then outsourcing enquiry handling to another company may be appropriate. If the required impression is of a company that values their customers because they take the time to answer any questions fully and are passionate about the business, then handling the enquiries in house is better. There are a number of good outsourced enquiry handling companies that do take the time to really understand the franchise business and assign a highly

> *The way the enquiry is handled is likely to be the first real impression a prospective franchisee will get of the brand*

competent person who can enthuse about the franchise and answer every question a person has fully. Equally there are a number of franchisors that do not handle enquiries effectively and use junior staff which will convey a poor image of the franchisor.

When deciding who is going to undertake each task in the enquiry handling process it is important to consider the enquiry handling objectives and decide who can best achieve these objectives.

Initial Enquiry Handling Plan

Having created the franchise enquiry handling objectives, identified what information will be processed at each stage of the initial enquiry handling process, decided when each task will take place, and who will do each task. This plan should be written down and everyone involved in the franchise should be aware of their involvement.

Monitoring and Evaluation

The Initial Enquiry Handling Plan however is only as good its implementation. Therefore it is important to have the systems and processes in place to monitor and evaluate how well the plan is being met. If it states that 100% of enquiries will be responded to within 30 minutes of receipt, a system is required that can record when every enquiry is received, and when the acknowledgment is sent. The system also needs to identify who needs to be sent a Franchise Brochure and a Franchise Brochure Covering Letter each day, as well as recording when they are actually sent. It will need to be able to record any specific question asked and the responses made. Finally the system needs to be able to "flag" when each person needs to be contacted, and record any comments from the enquirer.

The enquiry handling system does not necessarily need to be a computerised, although there are many software packages that are relatively inexpensive and easy to use. Whatever system is adopted it must allow the relevant person to undertake each task and record the outcomes. It must also generate a report to allow the person who takes ultimate responsibility for franchisee recruitment to review how well the enquiry handling processes are being handled.

Franchisee Interview

For those applicants that are sent the franchise brochure and on reviewing it believe that they may be suitable as a franchisee, they will be sent an application form. As previously discussed a typical Franchise Application Form will be made up of seven sections:

1. Detailed personal information about the applicant such as address, if they have a spouse or partner, children or dependents.
2. Educational background and qualifications.
3. Employment history which should show who they worked for and the roles they had in each job, and for how long.
4. Financial standing should indicate whether they would need to borrow to finance their franchise or they have the financial resources already, details of their bank for future references, and whether they have ever been declared a bankrupt.

5. Details of at least two people who will act as personal references.
6. Answers to questions about their suitability to be a franchisee and to carry out the franchisee role.
7. An opportunity for the applicant to provide any other relevant information that they would like the franchisor to consider.

The purpose of the Franchise Application Form is to provide the franchisor with sufficient information to decide whether the individual meets the franchisee profile and has the potential to be a franchisee. For those suitable people, the next step in the recruitment process is the franchise interview. The franchise interview will allow the franchisor to find out more about the applicant, decide whether the applicant has the skills and personality to be a successful franchisee, and to provide the applicant with all the information they will need to make an informed decision as to whether to become a franchisee or not.

> *The franchise interview will allow the franchisor to decide whether the applicant has the skills and personality to be a successful franchisee*

The franchise interview normally has five core components:

1. An opportunity for the franchisor to ask questions to clarify the applicant's responses on their application form and to ask additional questions to assess the applicant's suitability to become a franchisee.
2. Provide the applicant with all the information they need about the franchise so that they will be in a position to decide if the franchise is right for them.
3. An opportunity for the applicant to ask questions.
4. An opportunity for the applicant to see the franchisors office and meet the franchisors key staff.
5. To explain the post interview process.

Franchisor Questions

Dependent on the answers made by the applicant on the application form, the franchisor may wish to either ask questions to clarify the original answers or ask supplementary questions. This section of the interview is an opportunity for the franchisor to decide whether the applicant has all the qualities that they are looking for in their franchisees. These qualities may include having the technical ability to carry out the role of a franchisee successfully; having the drive and commitment to run their own franchised business, maximising the potential in the franchisee's territory; as well as having the right personality that will enable them to work with the franchisor and other members of the franchisee network.

The number of questions asked by the franchisor is entirely up to them. Ultimately, the franchisor should ask as many questions as they need, in order that they feel comfortable knowing whether the applicant would be a successful franchisee of theirs.

It is important that the franchisor asks their questions at the start of the interview and <u>before</u> they have been through the information on the franchise opportunity as the applicant may modify their answers to any questions, based on what the franchisor has already told them in the belief that it will be what the franchisor wants to hear rather than what the applicant necessarily believes.

Franchise Information

In order to enable the applicant to decide whether the franchise is right for them, they will need to be given information on all aspects of the franchise business. This information is normally provided in the form of the Franchise Disclosure Document, as previously described in the section on franchise recruitment material. The Franchise Disclosure Pack normally includes:

1. Background on the franchisor business.
2. An assessment of the market for the franchisors products and services.
3. Details relating to the Franchise Package; what it costs and what a franchisee gets for their money.

4. Details relating to terms of the franchise such as how long the franchise is for, what happens if a franchisee wants to renew, the ongoing fees a franchisee will pay, and the legal status that a franchisee must operate. It will also provide details on whether the franchisee will operate from home or commercial premises, whether a franchisee has to register for VAT before commencing their business, the policy regarding national accounts and many important terms relating to the franchise.

5. The Franchise territory criteria and whether franchises will be offered on an exclusive or non exclusive basis, and what this means in practice to the franchisee.

6. Any minimum performance requirements that the franchisee must meet such as minimum income levels, minimum local marketing spend, or any other minimum performance criteria relevant to the franchise.

7. The obligations that the franchisee must meet.

8. The obligations that the franchisor must meet.

9. The franchisee profile.

10. A SWOT analysis explaining what the Strengths, Weaknesses, Opportunities and Threats are to the franchise.

11. Detailed franchisee financial projections.

It is imperative that the applicant signs a Confidentiality Agreement before they are given the Franchise Disclosure Pack

At the franchisee interview, the franchisor will provide the applicant with a copy of the Franchise Disclosure Pack which they can write on and take away with them. Due to the confidential nature of the information contained within the Franchise Disclosure Pack, it is imperative that the applicant signs a confidentiality agreement before they are given the Franchise Disclosure Pack.

The Franchise Disclosure pack is usually constructed in a logical manner which enables the franchisor to go through it, page by page, during the interview. It is far better to go through each part of the Franchise Disclosure Pack with the applicant as it provides the franchisor with an opportunity to emphasise and elaborate on critical elements. Additionally by going through each section in detail, it allows the applicant to clarify specific aspects of the franchise and ask any supplementary questions.

Applicant Questions

If the Franchise Disclosure Pack is comprehensive and has been reviewed with the applicant page by page, most of the questions the applicant may have will have been answered.

It is very normal in franchise interviews that follow the process above, that at this stage the applicant will bring out a list of questions they prepared in advance of the interview. Having provided the applicant with such comprehensive information beforehand, the majority of the applicant's questions will already have been answered. This will give a positive impression of the franchisor.

Franchisor Premises and Key Staff
Prior to the interview, it is unlikely that the applicant will have seen the franchisor's Head Office or met the key staff in the business. The interview is an ideal opportunity to let the applicant see how the franchisor operates and the key staff that they will be dealing with should they become a franchisee.

Some smaller franchised businesses are often worried about the impression that their premises may have on an applicant. It is important for the long term relationship between the franchisor and the franchisee that an applicant knows the type of business they will be part of and they are happy with it. If a franchisor tries to hide parts of their business through a belief that the applicant will not being impressed with it, it will only lead to problems in the future as the franchisee will inevitably find out the truth at some point. It is far better that they find out before they become a franchisee than after the event.

Anyone who becomes a franchisee has to be prepared to fit in with the franchisor's environment and staff. If an applicant cannot "accept" the franchisor and their staff as they are, they are perhaps not suited to join as a franchisee!

Next Steps

The final part of the franchisee interview should explain what will happen after the interview. The franchisor needs to explain that within a certain timescale, such as seven days, they will write to the applicant either to offer a provisional offer, invite the applicant for a second interview, or inform them that they have been unsuccessful in their application to become a franchisee.

The franchisor must also explain what the applicant will need to do if they are offered a provisional offer and wish to accept it, or if they are invited to a second interview.

It is important that the applicant leaves the interview having been given all the information they need to have to be able to decide what to do if the franchisor makes them a provisional offer. It is also important that any timescales given by the franchisor are adhered to.

Additional Steps

I have explained a standard interview process however for some franchises additional steps will need to be included within the overall interview process. It may be that an applicant will be asked to undertake a role play as part of the interview process or go out with an existing franchisee to see what life as a franchisee is really like. Some franchisors will ask franchisees to attend a separate interview where they will need to present a franchise business plan to the franchisor.

Each franchisor should decide what their interview process should include and how it should be managed in order that they can assess the suitability of an applicant and provide all the information the applicant will need to make an informed judgement as to whether the franchise is right for them. Include additional steps in the interview process, if it will help. There are no rules for how long the interview process should last or what it should include.

Recruitment Processing

This part of the recruitment process deals with what happens when a franchisor decides to make a provisional franchise offer and the applicant accepts it. This process usually consists of seven parts:

1. Making the Franchise Provisional Offer
2. The applicant signing a Deposit Agreement and paying their deposit
3. The applicant being sent and reviewing the Franchise Agreement
4. The applicant asking questions about the Franchise Agreement

5. Taking references on the applicant
6. The franchisor issuing a Formal Franchise Offer
7. Signing the Franchise Agreement and paying the balance of the franchise cost

Provisional Offer

The franchisor sends the applicant a provisional offer for a franchise. It will state the franchise territory that the provisional offer relates to and the conditions linked to the provisional offer.

The usual conditions linked to provisional offers are:

- A time limit that the provisional offer will last, after which the offer is rescinded
- That a Deposit Agreement needs to be signed and deposit paid in order to accept the provisional offer

The franchisor usually states that if the applicant accepts the provisional offer, by signing the Deposit Agreement and paying their deposit, the franchisor will not take forward any other enquiries regarding the territory the provisional offer relates to. This provides the applicant with the necessary time to review the Franchise Agreement and whether to become a franchisee without undue pressure being applied.

The provisional offer usually takes the form of a letter from the franchisor together with a Deposit Agreement that will need to be signed should the applicant wish to accept the offer.

Deposit Agreement and Deposit Payment

The Deposit Agreement is a legal document that sets out the conditions under which the deposit is made. The applicant needs to sign the agreement and pay the specified deposit amount to the franchisor should they wish to accept the provisional offer.

The deposit is usually refundable less any direct costs

The deposit is usually refundable, should the applicant decide not to proceed with their application to become a franchisee, less any direct costs that the franchisor has incurred. Direct costs are referred to as those costs paid to third parties. That means that the franchisor cannot deduct an amount for their time in handling the application, but can deduct costs such as legal fees relating to sending out the Franchise Agreement or responding to an applicant's questions on the Franchise Agreement. Direct costs could also include travel costs should the franchisor need to visit the applicant after the deposit was made.

Franchise Agreement

Once the franchisor receives the signed Deposit Agreement and the deposit fee, they will then send the applicant the Franchise Agreement. The Franchise Agreement lays out all the terms under which the Franchise would be granted and the obligations for both franchisor and franchisee.

As previously mentioned, the Franchise Agreement should not be viewed as a negotiable document. It is important that every franchisee in the franchise network has the same Franchise Agreement. This not only prevents unrest amongst franchisees, whereby some will be aggrieved if their franchise was granted on worse terms than other franchisees, but also makes enforcement of the Franchise Agreement easier for the franchisor as everyone will have the same conditions they must abide to.

In order to prevent future problems, it is important that the applicant understands all the terms under which the Franchise is granted and the various obligations, before they sign. As with many legal agreements, franchise agreements are often very complex and can be difficult for people to fully understand. It is for this reason and to prevent undue concern and delay for the applicant, as well as unnecessary costs for both the franchisor and the applicant, that the Franchise Agreement is reviewed by a specialist franchise solicitor.

The applicant must understand all the terms under which the Franchise is granted before they sign

Franchising is a specialist area and unless the solicitor fully understands franchising, they may raise unnecessary concerns with the applicant. Therefore, despite specialist franchise solicitors being more expensive than most general solicitors, the additional cost is money well worth spending. Many franchisors will direct the applicant to the British Franchise Association website at www.thebfa.org for a list of accredited franchise solicitors from which to choose from.

Franchise Agreement Questions

As previously stated the Franchise Agreement is sent to the applicant so that they are aware of the terms under which the franchise is granted, and it is not open for negotiation. Despite this, many applicants still ask questions and try to get clauses changed to be more in their favour.

Franchisors should only amend clauses in the Franchise Agreement in exceptional circumstances

Franchisors should only amend clauses in the Franchise Agreement in exceptional circumstances. This is easier for established franchisors, however for new franchisors that are just starting out and want to recruit their first franchisees, there is a temptation to appease the applicant for fear of the applicant pulling out. If an applicant is not prepared to sign the standard agreement then it is probably best that they do not become a franchisee.

On rare occasions a franchisor may agree to a clause change in the Franchise Agreement or agree to an additional condition for the franchise. An example of the type of clause that might be changed would be where the Franchise Agreement states that the franchisee must devote their full time to their franchise business. The applicant may have an involvement in a non competing business, such as a business belonging to their spouse, and may need to spend a limited amount of time on that business. If the franchisor believes that this will not impact on the franchisee's ability to successfully run their franchise, they may accept a change to this clause. The change would be made through a side letter that accompanies the Franchise Agreement rather than changing the original wording, making reference to the original clause and the change that has been agreed.

There are also times when an applicant may wish to take an option to buy their neighbouring franchise territory. It is good practice that a franchisor does not sell a second franchise territory to a new franchisee until they have proved that they can successfully operate the first franchise territory. In this situation the franchisor may attach a side letter to the Franchise Agreement that gives the franchisee the first right on their neighbouring territory. Normally an agreement like this would come with certain terms such as: the franchisee must have operated successfully for at least nine months before they can purchase the second territory and that if an enquiry is made for the neighbouring territory before the nine months that the franchisor is permitted to sell the territory to another person. In addition it may state that if after nine months the franchisor receives an enquiry for the second territory and the franchisee is not in a position to, or doesn't want to buy the second territory within twenty eight days, that the territory can be sold to another person.

Having answered any questions on the Franchise Agreement raised by the applicant and dealt with any exceptional circumstances under a side letter, the franchisee should be in a position to sign the Franchise Agreement.

References

Before allowing the applicant to sign the Franchise Agreement, it is important that the franchisor takes references on the applicant. Although the franchisor may be sure that the applicant will make a good franchisee, it is worth taking the extra time to take references as this will be the last opportunity the franchisor has to check they are making the right decision.

The franchisor should write to the people listed as referees on the franchise application form, explaining that they are considering offering the applicant a franchise. The franchisor should explain the role the applicant will be required to undertake as a franchisee and ask the referees to confirm the involvement they have had with the applicant and ask for their own personal assessment of the applicant's suitability for the role of a franchisee.

Formal Offer

Once the applicants questions have been answered, any exceptional changes are dealt with, and the franchisor receives suitable references, the franchisor will be in a position to issue the Formal Franchise Offer.

The Formal Offer Letter will make the provisional offer formal and will explain the process that the applicant needs go through to accept the formal offer.

Signing the Franchise Agreement

The final stage in the franchise recruitment process is for the applicant to sign the Franchise Agreement and pay the franchise fee less any deposit payment that has been made.

The Franchise Agreement will require both the applicant and the franchisor to sign. The applicant will need to have their signature witnessed which can be done either by a third party or a member of the franchisor's staff, so long as it is not the same person that signs the agreement on behalf of the franchisor.

The franchisor should keep one signed copy of the Franchise Agreement and give the franchisee a signed copy for their own records. Once the Franchise Agreement has been signed and the franchise fee received, the applicant will formally become a franchisee.

Amendments to the Standard Recruitment Process

As previously stated, some franchisors will not issue a Provisional Offer or require applicants to sign a Deposit Agreement or pay any deposit, preferring instead to send a copy of the Franchise Agreement to those applicants interviewed who the franchisor believes are suitable as franchisees.

This approach has the advantage of simplifying the recruitment process by cutting out steps in the recruitment process. The disadvantage is that the applicant does not have to indicate any level of commitment right up until the time they sign the Franchise Agreement. This can lead to a higher drop out rate by applicants at the last moment which will waste the franchisor's time and may result in new enquiries for territories under consideration being lost.

Chapter 13

FRANCHISEE TRAINING & SET-UP

Once a person has signed the Franchise Agreement and paid their franchise fees, the last step in the franchise recruitment process is getting the franchisee ready to start trading. This will involve training the franchisee in all aspects of the franchise business as well getting the franchisee set-up to start trading,

Franchisee Training

The most critical step in ensuring that a franchisee is going to be successful and operate according to the rules of the franchisor, is the franchisee training. The content, length and format of the franchisee training will vary for each franchise regardless as to what franchise it is; franchisee training will cover three areas:

1. How to run a business
2. The technical elements of the product or service the franchisee will sell
3. Franchise specific requirements

Part 1 – How to Run a Business

The whole nature of franchising is that the franchisees run their own businesses. This means that regardless as to what product or service their business sells, franchisees will need to understand how to run a successful business.

Many people who become franchisees have not run a business before, therefore it is important that the franchisor provides appropriate training. For franchisees, this business training should cover four key elements:

- Finance
- Legal and Compliance
- Staff
- Back Office Systems

Finance

It is important that franchisees are trained on the importance of having up-to-date financial information and how to use and interpret the information for the benefit of the business. In many franchises, franchisees are either discouraged or prevented from doing their own bookkeeping. This is because franchisors want their franchisees to spend as much of their time as possible focused on income generating tasks. A number of franchisors will do the bookkeeping for their franchisees, which of course they charge for. Others will coordinate an outsourced chargeable bookkeeping service, whilst others leave it up to the franchisee to source their own local bookkeepers. Whichever approach is taken, franchisees should spend their time analysing the financial reports produced by their bookkeepers so that they understand at all times, how their business is performing and what actions need to be taken to address any weaknesses in the financial performance of the business. The franchisee training should focus on how to interpret financial reports and how to identify strengths and weaknesses in the financial performance of the business so that appropriate action can be taken. Many of the customer management software systems used by franchisors will create reports on all aspects of a franchisee's business.

Compliance

There are many legal, regulatory and general business requirements that a franchise business, like any other business needs to undertake and comply with. These requirements can include:

- Creating the legal entity that the business is going to trade under, such as Sole Trader, Partnership or Limited Company.
- Informing the relevant authorities that the business has been created.

- Registering for VAT and filing VAT returns.
- Registering as a data controller to comply with the Data Protection Act.
- Taking out the necessary insurance required by the franchise business.
- Setting up a business bank account and other banking services.

Many franchisees will not have experienced any of the above before. It is therefore important that the franchisor provides training in all these aspects, enabling each franchisee to set-up correctly from the outset. On the subject of training the franchisee, the training does not have to be done by the franchisor, it is perfectly acceptable, and often better, that certain training is undertaken by external professionals.

Staff

A number of franchises will require the franchisee to employ staff. Where this is the case, the franchisee will need to be trained on how to effectively advertise for, recruit, train and manage their staff. If all the franchisees in a network are going to operate in the same way, it is important that the staff that operate in the franchise business, are the right people to do the job, have been trained to do the job, and are managed correctly. The franchisee will also need training on how to comply with employment law covering areas such as job descriptions and employment contracts.

In a number of franchises, all staff must be trained and accredited by the franchisor, in others the training is left to the franchisee. Whichever approach is taken, the franchisee must be trained to understand the process to follow and if they are to train their own staff, how this training should be undertaken.

Finally, if a franchise is going to be successful they will need to know how to manage their staff correctly. This may include how to communicate with staff effectively, how to monitor staff performance and give feedback, what to do when issues arise and how to motivate and get the best out of their staff.

A number of franchisors may make membership of an external employment advisory service a condition of the franchise

A number of franchisors may make membership of an external employment advisory service a condition of the franchise. This way the franchisee will be able to access professional employment advice at any time, ensuring that they comply with current employment legislation. Other franchisors will provide ongoing advice to their franchisees with regards to employment advice. Whatever approach is taken it is of paramount importance that the franchisee understands what the legal requirements when employing staff and fully understand the policies and procedures that the franchisor wishes them to follow in the training and management of their staff.

Back Office Systems

For most franchises, the franchisee will be required to use the same proven back office systems and process as used by the franchisor. These back office systems will vary from franchise to franchise, however if a franchisee is going to use the systems correctly, they will require training.

Some franchisors use systems that have been specifically created for themselves. In these cases it will either be down to the franchisor to train the franchisee or the company that developed the systems in the first place. Where a franchise uses systems that are more generic and common place, it is normal that the franchisor will provide basic training on the system, and where a franchisee wishes to know more, they will be left to source additional training from an external source, at their own cost.

Whichever approach to system training a franchisor adopts, it should be supported by a detailed user manual. This can either be incorporated within the Franchise Operations Manual, or can be a stand alone manual. It is unrealistic to expect any franchisee to remember absolutely everything they are taught on their training course and therefore all training must be supported by a user manual that the franchisee can refer to, as necessary.

Part 2 – The Technical Elements

This section of the franchisee training is concerned with how to sell and deliver the products and services of the franchised business. This technical element of the training is normally broken down into three parts:

- How to market the products and services of the business.
- How to sell the products and service of the business.
- How to deliver/install the products and services.

How to Market

When a person buys a franchise they are buying into a proven business model. This proven model will include how to effectively market the products and services of the business. If no one knows that the franchised business exists or are not aware of the different products and services that it sells, it is rather unrealistic to expect that the business will be successful.

In most businesses, franchised or not, there are a wide range of different ways that the products or services of the business could be marketed. Business owners over the years will try different marketing mediums to greater or lesser success. This is the same for the franchisor. Not every bit of marketing they may have tried over the years will have worked. When someone buys a franchise they are buying into the knowledge and experience of the franchisor, this includes the most effective ways to market the businesses products and services. Training in the most effective ways to market their business, the franchisee is likely to waste money trying various marketing approaches that have historically proven ineffective.

When training a franchisee on how best to market in their territory it is important to understand that the marketing undertaken will need to be adjusted to take into account local factors. A franchisor may have had little success in the past with advertising their services in local papers or at local networking groups. However it may be that in a certain franchise territory there is a very good local paper and very good local networking groups. Conversely, the franchisor may have had success will local radio advertising however in the franchisee's territory, the local radio station is not very good. It is for this reason that the franchisee training should include a section on what marketing has worked in the franchisors experience however part of the franchisee training should include how to research and evaluate the different marketing media in their own local area. The franchisee should develop their own local marketing plan based on what they have learnt from the franchisor together with their own local research. The franchisee then shares this with the franchisor so that they can provide feedback and advice prior to the franchisee implementing their local marketing plan.

The franchisee should develop their own local marketing plan

How to Sell

All franchisors will have developed systems and processes on how to sell to customers. These will include what happens when a customer lead is received, through to how to turn the lead into a sale. Every franchise is different; therefore the sales process for an oven cleaning franchise will be very different from a commercial cleaning contract sale. Whatever the business is, the franchisee needs to be trained in the successful sales process of the franchisor.

A common mistake made by some franchisors is that they train their franchisees on the technical nature of the business, such as all the different types of blinds and awnings that the franchisee can sell. However they then leave it up to the franchisee to sell in their own way. There are two key problems with this approach:

Firstly the franchisee may not be very good at selling. If this is the case then the franchisee is likely to covert less of the enquiries into actual sales, affecting their profitability which in turn will affect the franchisor, either in the franchisor fees where they are directly linked to the franchisees sales, or for future franchisee recruitment. This is because most prospective franchisees are advised to speak to the existing franchisees within a network and it is likely to put a person off buying a franchise if they talk of failing or struggling franchisee.

Secondly, there is a risk to the brand integrity if franchisees are allowed to sell however they like. If a network has ten franchisees and they are all allowed to sell as they want, it is likely that all ten will adopt slightly different methods. Of course some sales methods may be very good and effective however there may be some that either are ineffective of worse still, damage the reputation of the franchisor's brand. The last thing a franchisor wants is their brand associated with bad or unethical selling methods such as one sees on "Rogue Trader" television programmes. This type of bad publicity can ruin a franchise. The only way to prevent this type of situation from happening is to train every franchisee how to sell using the franchisor's proven method way and then monitor them to ensure that they are selling the way they have been trained.

The last thing a franchisor wants is their brand associated with bad or unethical selling methods

How to Deliver and Install

For virtually every franchise, once the franchisee has sold a product or service they will need to deliver or install it. If a franchisee sells a corporate training course, it is likely that they will have to run the training course for the customer. If a franchisee has a fast food take away business, when customers place orders the franchisee needs to make sure it is cooked and presented to the customers in exactly the same way every time and in the same way that every other franchisee in the network does.

This element of the technical training is normally the most extensive part of the franchisees training. The franchisee will need to know every part of the delivery and installation process if they are going to deliver and install the product or service in exactly the same way, every time. For a franchise that cleans and sweeps chimneys, the franchisee will need to know every piece of equipment that they will need, how to set each piece up, and how to operate the equipment. In addition they will need to know how to deal with any issues or problems that can occur, how to check the cleaning has been done properly and how to tidy up after themselves. A flower arranging franchise will need to know all the different flowers that can be used, the sizes of arrangements that can be made, how to arrange the flowers, how to package them and how to deliver the flowers to the customer.

The technical training is normally the most extensive part of the franchisee training

In order that all franchisees deliver and install the products and services they sell in exactly the same way every time, they must be fully trained. They must also have a detailed instruction manual covering every part of the process so that they can refer to it any time required. If you go to McDonald's you know, love the product or not, that the Big Mac will taste the same whichever McDonald's you visit. Franchisors need to train franchisees so that whichever franchisee delivers the products or services, and wherever in the county they are, the customer will always get the same consistent result.

Part 3 - Franchise Specific Requirements

In franchising, unlike most traditional businesses, franchise businesses have a unique extra element to them. This involves the franchisee reporting back to the franchisor on their performance and paying a variety of franchise fees to the franchisor.

Franchisees will need to be given training on what reports are required and the frequency they must provide them. Some franchises, such as those in the fast foods industry, often require franchisees to report back to the franchisor on a weekly basis. Other franchises only require franchisees to report back on a monthly basis. Whatever frequency is chosen, the reason for franchisee feedback should be twofold:

1. To know how the franchisee is performing so that the franchisor can give support, advice and where necessary additional training to help the franchisee improve.

2. To know what fees to charge the franchisee. Many franchisor fees are based on a percentage of the franchisee's turnover. Where this is the

case the franchisor will need to know their turnover to calculate the fees.

The franchisee needs to be trained in what information they will need to provide to the franchisor, the frequency they need to provide it and in what format. A fast food franchise may require more extensive reports, and more frequently from their franchisees than a dog grooming franchise. Whatever level and frequency of reporting adopted, it is important to make it simple for the franchisee to provide it.

There are some software systems that will create this information automatically for the franchisee. Other reports are partly automated and partly rely on the franchisee completing a manual return. If the franchisee is going to have to complete a manual return it is important that they understand why the information is required. If it is explained to the franchisees that there is a certain conversion rate that is expected within the business and any rate lower than the normal would indicate a potential issue, and that it is only through knowing that an issue exists can the franchisor help, then most franchisees would feel that is reasonable to provide this information. If however the franchisee is asked to report on the type and make of every car they wash in their car washing franchisee, but there is no explanation of why this is required, then it is likely that some of the franchisees won't provide all the information and possibly make some of it up.

I am sure that franchisors will turn to their Franchise Agreement and say that the franchisee must do exactly as they are told as the Franchise Agreement says so, however would you want to have unhappy and disgruntled franchisees when there is no need? Happy, motivated franchisees are like happy motivated staff, far easier to manage and far more likely to perform than unhappy disgruntled ones.

> *Happy, motivated franchisees are far easier to manage and far more likely to perform*

If there is a reason to collect information explain it to the franchisees. If there is no reason to collect the information then don't. However whatever is asked for, franchisees will need to be trained how to collect the information, how to collate it and in what format and when and how to submit it.

Training Summary

When it comes to franchisee training, the only way on ensuring that every franchisee in the franchise network runs their business exactly as they should, is by providing them with detailed training supported by a comprehensive Franchise Operations Manual and other related guides that they can refer to.

SECTION 4

Franchising
In Operation

Section Four will look at what happens once a franchise has been launched and franchisees are recruited. It will show how to successfully manage a franchise network, franchising internationally, and selling a franchised business. These three areas are extensive and complex topics in their own right and in this book I will only be able to briefly highlight some of the key elements within each area that are useful for business owners to be aware of when considering franchising.

The three areas that I will discuss in summary are:

Chapter 14 - Franchisee Management
This chapter will cover the importance of managing franchisees and three key methods for franchisors to effective manage their franchisee network.

Chapter 15 - Franchising Internationally
This chapter will cover some of the main influencing factors for franchisors who may wish to franchise internationally.

Chapter 16 - Franchise Sales
The final chapter will cover the topic of franchise sales, both for franchisees and the franchisor.

Chapter 14

FRANCHISEE MANAGEMENT

For any franchisor business to be successful, the hard work really starts once franchisees are recruited and trained. Unfortunately for some franchisors they view it the other way round and believe that once they have recruited and trained their franchisees they can sit back and watch the money start to roll in.

Throughout his book there has been reference to the importance of having a network of successful franchisees all operating their franchised businesses in the same way. When anyone attends a training course on any topic, nobody would expect the attendee to remember absolutely everything they were taught. Even with supporting training guides that a person can refer to at a later stage, it would be unrealistic to expect anyone to operate and get everything correct. Franchise training is no different. The initial franchisee training and the supporting franchise operations manual is only the first step in having franchisees that all operate successfully in exactly the same way. The training and franchise operations manual need to be supported by:

1. Regular performance monitoring
2. Ongoing training
3. Regular communication

Regular Performance Monitoring

In order for a franchisor to know if all of their franchisees are operating in exactly the same way and in compliance with the terms of the Franchise Agreement and the instructions within the Franchise Operations Manual, they need to instigate a range of systems and processes to enable them to monitor what their franchisees are doing.

In the last chapter the contractual obligations of the franchisee were discussed. To assist the franchisee management process, the franchisee will have a contractual responsibility as specified in both the Franchise Agreement and the Franchise Operations

One of the big mistakes made by franchisors is relying purely on the franchisee reports to monitor their franchisee's performance

Manual to provide certain information at a specified time to the franchisor about their business. This enables the franchisor to remotely monitor a franchisee's performance and identify any issues that may need addressing. This however should only be one part of performance monitoring undertaken by the franchisor.

One of the big mistakes made by franchisors is relying purely on the weekly or monthly franchisee reports to monitor their franchisee's performance. Unfortunately these weekly and monthly reports are only as good as the information they contain. Where a franchisee report is completed manually, they can intentionally or unintentionally omit certain information that will mean that the franchisor does not have a true picture of how they are performing. Even automated franchisee reporting systems are open to abuse. A franchisee may decide to not record information that they may believe will reflect badly on them. Therefore any good franchisee performance monitoring system must substantiate any franchise reports with independent verification processes. These processes could involve monthly franchisor visits to observe the franchisee in action, or may involve independent mystery shopping exercises or independent audits. Whatever verification processes are adopted, they must, together with the franchisee's reports enable the franchisor to have an accurate picture of exactly how the franchisee is performing. Franchisors can only help their franchisees if they know the true picture.

Ongoing Training

Ongoing training is an essential part of any successful franchise operation and is used for three main reasons:

- Addressing knowledge gaps
- Reinforcing key points
- Learning new skills

Addressing Knowledge Gaps

Addressing gaps in the franchisee's knowledge, as identified through the performance monitoring systems and processes, is probably the most obvious reason for undertaking ongoing franchisee training. As previously stated, it is unreasonable to expect anyone to remember absolutely everything they are taught on a training course. Even with supporting manuals and guides for a franchisee to refer to doesn't guarantee that a franchisee will perform every task the way it should be. A franchisee may incorrectly think they remember how they were taught to do a task and therefore not check whether they are doing it right. Alternatively a franchisee may refer to a manual or guide to check that they are doing a task correctly only to misinterpret the instructions in the manual. Although franchise manuals and guides should be written in a way to try ensure that they are simple to understand and minimise the risk of misinterpretation, people will always make mistakes. Therefore ongoing training can be used to address any gaps and misunderstandings in the franchisees knowledge.

Reinforcing Key Points

There may also be certain key parts of a franchise business that franchisees may need to be reminded of, for instance the unique selling points compared with their competitors. The franchisor must ensure that franchisees do not cut corners and omit to do this, if it makes the business stand out. A franchisee running a car washing business may believe that it is more important to get to the cars that are queuing to be cleaned as quickly as possible rather than spend the extra couple of minutes cleaning the inside door sills, especially as they will charge the same amount regardless. It may be that the franchisee's monthly report may not identify this failing or it may be that when the franchisor visits, the franchisee is not busy and therefore does the job as they should. In these instances getting franchisees together to reinforce the importance of key parts of the business is critical. Not only can you reinforce these key points but it will allow you to address any issues raised by your franchisees. It may be that a franchisee disagrees with the importance of doing the extra task or key point and this will allow you to address their concern.

Often when ongoing reinforcement training is undertaken in groups of franchisees at the same time, other franchisees will reinforce the benefit of doing the task properly. This is the benefit of regular reinforcement training.

Learning New Skills

When a person buys a franchise they are usually entering a long term commitment. Typically, franchises are for five years with options to renew. Many franchises are longer than this. This means that it is likely that a franchisee will be operating their business for at least ten years. If a franchisor looks at the products and services they offer today and compare back to what was offered ten years ago, there are likely to have been changes made. Any business that is going to remain competitive needs to react to changes in market conditions. Franchise businesses, as with any other business need to continually look at ways to improve what they are offer. In a franchise, this research and development role is undertaken by the franchisor. The franchisor should develop and test new products, services and procedures and when they are ready role them out through their franchisee network. Naturally as this will be new, the franchisee will need training on the new product or service. The franchisor then has to ensure that they bring their franchisees together to explain the reasons for the new products, service or procedure and then train them on their use.

Regular Communication

The final part of franchise management covered in this book is a brief overview of the importance of regular communication. As with any relationship, whether it is between boss and employee, family members or franchisor and franchisee, regular communication is essential.

For a franchise to be successful it is essential that the franchisor and franchisee work together towards a common goal. The franchisee needs to believe that the franchisor has their best interest at heart and in doing so they are likely to be more motivated in the way they run their franchise, as opposed to feeling they are working alone without any support or interest from their franchisor.

> *For a franchise to be successful the franchisor and franchisee must work together towards a common goal*

Regular communication also provides opportunities for issues to be voiced and addressed at an early stage before they escalate into a bigger issue. Although some franchisees may believe that regular communication with their franchisor is unnecessary and too time consuming and takes them away from their business, it is the franchisors contractual responsibility to help and support their franchisees. If the franchisor is going to be effective in the help and support they provide their franchisees then they must have regular contact with them.

Regular communication doesn't necessarily mean face to face meetings. Face to face meetings are an excellent way of communicating however telephone calls, emails, circulars and even texting can be good ways of maintaining contact between franchisors and franchisees. A telephone call just to see how a franchisee is doing may just provide the opportunity for a franchisee to raise an issue causing them concern. It is an easy option to assume the franchisee has the franchisors contact details and therefore will make contact if they have a problem. In realty, often franchisees do not feel issues are big enough to warrant contacting their franchisor about however, if not addressed the issue is unlikely to go away and will more likely fester and grow. By having regular contact with their franchisees, franchisors will provide the opportunity for issues to be raised and be resolved, freeing the franchisee to return to running their franchised business without the "issues" holding them back.

Franchisee Management Summary

Although I have only touched on a couple areas within the whole topic of franchisee management the one message that should be clear is that when successfully franchising a business, the hard work really starts when the franchisees are recruited and continues with their ongoing management.

Chapter 15

FRANCHISING INTERNATIONALLY

For many companies, franchising internationally is a very appealing thought. As there are already a number of books dedicated to the subject of how to franchise internationally, I will only cover a few very general points that may be helpful for people to be aware of even before they start franchising domestically.

The four important elements in relation to franchising a business internationally that I am going to cover in brief are:

1. International franchise legislation
2. International franchise models
3. Tailoring for international markets
4. Local expertise

International Franchise Legislation

I have already mentioned that in the UK there is no specific franchise legislation. Instead franchising is covered by Standard Commercial Law. This however is not always the case in other countries. Many countries have legislation that covers the preregistration and filing of a franchise with local or national authorities before a franchisor may enter into discussions with prospective franchisees. Others have withholding tax laws that puts a levy on the fees earned by non domestic franchisors. Virtually all countries will have their own systems for registering Trade Marks and Patents in their countries. Understanding the various legislation that is involved in different countries makes international franchising both complex and costly. This is not to deter people from considering international franchising as the rewards both reputational and financial, can be immense, rather it is important to make people aware of scale of the work required to successfully franchise abroad.

In the section I will look at three important areas within international franchise legislation:

- Disclosure laws
- Withholding Tax
- Trade marks

Franchise Disclosure Laws

Many countries have different legislation governing franchising. Countries such as the UK govern franchising under their Standard Commercial Legislation whilst other countries have specific franchise laws. There are six European countries that have enacted a franchise disclosure law; they are Belgium, France, Italy, Romania, Spain and Sweden. In addition there are a number of countries that have general "good faith" type laws that can give rise to franchise disclosure obligations ("Good Faith Laws") and they are Germany, Austria, Portugal and Lithuania.

Whilst countries with "Good Faith Laws" rely on the general principle that parties owe to each other a duty of good faith and fair dealing during pre-contractual negotiations and do not list the items to be disclosed, countries with franchise disclosure laws provide a specific list of disclosure items. In all European disclosure law countries except Italy the franchisor is required to make two distinctly different types of disclosure. Firstly, the franchisor is expected to summarise certain important contractual provisions ("Contract Summaries"). Secondly, the franchisor is required to make certain commercial disclosures ("Commercial Disclosures").

Listed below is information relating to a number of different countries. Given the summary nature of the information provided below and because legislation can change, it is important that the information provided is only used to illustrate the differences between franchise disclosure requirements in different countries and that anyone considering franchising internationally seeks professional advice first.

France

The Loi Doubin of 31st December 1989 was the first European Franchise Disclosure law. It applies before the parties enter into an agreement that involves the exclusive or "semi-exclusive" right to use a trade name, trade mark or sign. The Loi Doubin applies to franchise agreements as the Franchisor usually grants to the franchisee the right to use a trade mark and certain proprietary signage. Additionally, there is semi exclusivity as most franchisors will impose a non competition obligation on the franchisee and grant to the franchisee an exclusive territory. Under article 1 of the Loi Doubin a disclosure document containing specified information must be given to the franchisee 20 days before signature of the contract. No deposit can be taken from the franchisee before the expiry of the 20 day period.

In France the Contract Summary must contain an overview of a number of important contractual provisions. This draws key clauses in the franchise agreement to the attention of the franchisee. The mandatory provisions required to be disclosed under the Law of 31 December 1989 are the term and the renewal conditions, the termination provisions, the transfer clause and the scope of exclusivity granted.

The Commercial Disclosure which must be made in France is as follows. The franchisor must provide details regarding the company that grants the franchise and its directors as well as banking references and a summary of the professional experience of the managers. The Franchisor must also provide copies of its accounts for the previous two years.

Belgium

Belgium has a history of giving the "weaker" party in third party relationships, such as exclusive distribution networks, a high level of protection. However, until February 2006 there was no legislation in Belgium specifically dealing with franchise disclosure.

The new Belgian franchise law came into effect on 1 February 2006. It applies to what is called "commercial partnerships". A commercial partnership is defined as an "agreement made between two persons where one person grants to the other the use of a commercial formula, a common sign, the transfer of know-how and commercial or technical assistance". A franchise typically involves the use of certain confidential know-how in connection with the sale of goods or the provision of services under a common trade mark. It follows that most franchise systems can be classified as "commercial partnerships".

In Belgium, the franchisor must summarise the obligations of the parties and state the consequences of not meeting these obligations. It must also provide a description of the non-compete clauses and all exclusive rights granted. These disclosure items are directed towards the provision of a "Contract Summary". The Franchisor must also highlight the grounds available to it for early termination of the franchise. This is of great practical significance as most franchise agreements contain numerous termination provisions giving the franchisor the right to terminate the franchise early. If those termination clauses are not summarised accurately in the disclosure document, they will not be enforceable. Any rights of first refusal or a purchase option(s) in favour of the franchisor and the rules as to the value assessment of the business when these rights are invoked must be given in the Contract Summary. Finally, it must summarise the conditions which apply to a renewal of the franchise.

The Commercial Disclosure must cover the name and address of the franchisor. If the franchisor is a legal entity, the identity and capacity of the persons representing the franchisor has to be given. The franchisor must also summarise the nature of the activities of the franchisor and the Intellectual Property rights that can be used by the franchisee. The franchisor's annual accounts for the last three years must also be provided. A summary of the historic development of the franchised network and the number of franchisees has to be given. This includes statistics on joiners and leavers.

Italy

Italian Law no. 129 "Regulation on franchising" which came into force on 25th, May 2004 regulates certain aspects of franchising in Italy. The law regulates various aspects of franchising including disclosure however Italian law requires no "Contract Summary". It simply requires that a copy of the written contract must be provided to the franchisee. In addition the contract must contain provisions that deal with the certain key items. The contract must address the exact amount of the franchise fee and investment that the franchisee is required to make and the method of payment of royalties. Where the franchisee is expected to achieve a certain minimum turnover the contract must address this. It must also address the exclusive territory granted to the franchisee (if any). The contract must further contain a description of the know how and a description of the services to be provided by the franchisor, such as technical and commercial assistance, planning and training. Finally the contractual conditions relevant to the renewal, termination and the transferability of the contract must be clearly set out in it. A well drafted Franchise Agreement will contain this information.

The law imposes a commercial disclosure obligation on the Franchisor. At least 30 days before the date of execution of the franchise contract, the franchisor must deliver to the franchisee a definitive draft of the contract together with a disclosure document containing certain commercial information. The document must set out certain corporate information relating to the franchisor. When requested by the franchisee, the franchisor's balance sheets for the three previous financial years must be provided.

Documentation relevant to the franchisor's trade marks must be disclosed and a description of the characteristic elements of the franchisor's commercial system must be given. Similar to France and Belgium, a list of all the franchisees belonging to franchisor's network must be made available and an indication of any fluctuations in the number of franchisees during the previous three years must be given. Similar to US disclosure item 3 of the Uniform Franchise Disclosure Document (UFDD) issued by the Federal Trade Commission applicable from 1st July 2008, which is acceptable in all fifty states; a concise description of any judicial lawsuits or arbitral procedures filed against the franchisor in the previous three years is also required. Most of these requirements are straight forward for both domestic and international franchisors to comply with.

Romania

Romania was one of the first Eastern European countries to adopt franchise specific legislation. On 28th August 1997 the Romanian Government issued Ordinance 52/ 1997 ("the Ordinance") on the legal regime applicable to franchising. The Ordinance sets out what a franchise agreement should include and the type of information which has to be disclosed to prospective franchisees during the pre-contractual phase.

The reason for this is to enable the franchisee to make an informed decision when entering into the franchise relationship. However, the Ordinance does not stipulate an exact time period within which the franchisor has to disclose the information to the prospective franchisee. One assumes that a reasonable period has to expire before a binding contract is made so as to enable the franchisee to evaluate the information provided.

The franchisor is expected to summarise the financial provisions of the contract namely the provisions setting out the initial fee, ongoing system fees like royalties, cost of advertising or carrying out services and taxes. Also the duration of the franchise agreement, conditions for renewal, termination and transfer of the agreement have to be disclosed. Details of any restrictions on the source of products or services have to be provided. Similar to Italy, the franchise agreement must also have a certain mandatory minimum content. Under Article 5 of the Ordinance, the contract must address the following:

- the object of the contract
- the rights and obligations of the parties
- the financial conditions
- the term of the contract
- the modification, extension or termination of the contract

Romanian law expects franchisors to make certain commercial disclosures. These are similar in nature to the disclosure items already encountered in France and Belgium. The franchisor must provide the name of the franchisor and a summary of the know-how that will be shared with the franchisee. They must also give information on the type of exclusivity granted and the size of the exclusive area. Finally, and importantly the franchisor is expected to disclose certain data which will enable the franchisee to evaluate the total investment costs.

Spain

Franchising in Spain is regulated by Law 7/1996 regarding Retail Commerce and Royal Decree 2485/1998. There are also certain rules and principles (including agency laws), contained in the Spanish Civil Code and Commercial Code.

The law defines franchising as follows: "A company, (the franchisor), assigns to another, (the franchisee), the right to exploit a franchise for the marketing of certain types of products or services, which includes the use of a common sign and a uniform layout of premises communication of know-how and the ongoing provision of commercial or technical assistance."

Article 62 of the law requires franchisor to deliver a pre-contractual disclosure document at least 20 days prior to the execution of a contract or the payment of a fee. The disclosure document must be in Writing and be "accurate and non-deceiving".

Since a franchise agreement is not a "categorised" agreement it is possible for parties to include whichever clauses they wish provided it complies with the basic contractual requirements contained in the Civil Code and Commercial Code. Article 1261 of the Spanish Civil Code 1889 requires that for a contract to be valid there has to be consent of all the contracting parties, a determined object has to form the subject matter of the contract and consideration for the undertaking is established.

A wide range of commercial data must be disclosed to the franchisee in Spain. The information must include franchisor's statutory identification data such as filing details, register number, capitalisation and a description of the franchisor's experience, starting with the date the franchisor company was incorporated and describing the different phases of the franchise network's development. In addition, a general description of the franchise (describing the system, the know-how and the technical assistance that the franchisor will provide) must be given.

Furthermore the franchisor must provide proof of ownership or licence to use the relevant Intellectual Property rights. Like in Italy, Belgium and France the size of the franchisors distribution network must be given listing both franchised and corporate outlets. Finally an estimate of the investment that the franchisee will have to make has to be given.

Sweden

The Disclosure Act 2006 came into force on 1st October 2006. It sets out a requirement to disclose certain information a reasonable period of time before a franchise agreement is entered into. Some have suggested that a reasonable period of time would be 14 days.

Similar to most other disclosure countries Sweden requires that the franchisor makes available a "Contract Summary". The Swedish legislation has identified which contractual provisions are considered of such importance that they must be brought to the particular attention of the franchisee by way of disclosure. These are:

1. Information on in term and post term non compete clauses that are contained in the franchise agreement
2. Information on the term, the conditions for amendment, renewal or termination
3. The financial consequences in case of termination
4. Information on how disputes in relation to the contract are to be resolved and the provisions on liability for costs in relation to such a dispute.

The requirement to summarize "the financial consequence of termination" is unusual. As most franchise agreements will not contain specific provisions detailing the financial consequences of termination it appears that this requirement goes beyond a mere summary of what is already in the contract.

The franchisor must provide a description of the franchise together with certain information on other system franchisees and the scope of their operations. Information on the fee to be paid by the franchisee and other financial terms must be set out in the disclosure document. Information on the categories of goods or services that the franchisee is required to purchase must also be given. Finally, as in Spain, information regarding the intellectual property rights that are the subject of the franchise must be given.

Non European Countries

In many non European countries, disclosure of various franchising documents is mandatory, a few examples of which are provided below:

The United States has one of the most comprehensive disclosure requirements, with the Federal Trade Commission (FTC) Rule on Disclosure Requirements and Prohibitions Concerning Franchising and Business Opportunity Ventures regulating the information a franchisor is required to supply the prospective franchisee. The FTC Rule applies in all fifty states and is intended to provide a minimum protection and applies wherever states have not adopted more stringent requirements.

In Australia the Franchising Code of Conduct imposes comprehensive disclosure requirements, a requirement for the mandatory mediation of franchising disputes and minimum standards for franchise agreements.

In Japan the Japan Fair Trade Commission (JFTC), the competition authority of Japan, published guidelines on franchising which consist of three parts: a general description of franchising; provisions for the disclosure of necessary information at the time of the offer of a franchise; and a part on vertical restraints between a franchisor and its franchisees.

In Brazil, there is a law relating to franchising contracts and other measures which deals mainly with disclosure, specifying the information that the franchisor should provide the franchisee with.

In India franchisors must provide a Uniform Franchising Offer Circular (UFOC) to anyone looking to buy a franchise and it is based on the US Franchise Disclosure Document (FDD).

Withholding Tax

The second area within international franchise legislation that will be covered relates to withholding tax as there are a number of countries and states that apply withholding tax levies on international franchisors.

In Saudi Arabia, international franchisors are liable for 20% withholding tax.

In India royalties paid by the franchisee to the franchisor for the use of the franchisor's intellectual property rights, are subject to tax at 20% on gross amount paid.

In Canada, the Canadian Income Tax Act imposes a withholding tax of 25% of any payment by a Canadian to a non-resident in regards to royalties or other similar payments.

It is therefore very important that any franchisor considering franchising internationally is aware whether withholding taxes apply as this may have dramatic effects on the profitability of the franchise. There are of course ways to limit the amount of withholding tax a franchisor pays however that is the realm of specialist accountants.

International Trade Marking

The final area within international franchise legislation that will be covered relates to international Trade Marks.

The importance of protecting Intellectual Property has already been discussed, which includes amongst other things Trade Marks and Patents. To sell someone the right to trade under a brand name or use a patented product or design in their business, they must first own the rights to them. In the UK, Trade Marks and Patents are registered through the Intellectual Property Office www.ipo.gov.uk. However this will normally only provide cover in the UK.

A Community Trade Mark registration gives protection in all member states of the European Union

In relation to Trade Marking, if looking to franchise internationally in Europe, one can apply for a Community Trade Mark (CTM) that negates the need to Trade Mark separately in each country. The great benefit of this is that one registration gives protection in all 27 member states of the European Union, rather than having to apply in each individual member state to obtain the same geographical coverage. Therefore, applying for a CTM can frequently prove an attractive option

The Madrid system is the primary international system for facilitating the registration of trademarks in multiple jurisdictions around the world

where a business seeks to operate in one or more European Union member states.

When international Trade Mark registration is required for countries outside Europe, the Madrid system for the international registration of marks, also conveniently known as the Madrid system or simply Madrid, is the primary international system for facilitating the registration of trademarks in multiple jurisdictions around the world. The Madrid system provides a centrally administered system of obtaining a bundle of trademark registrations in separate jurisdictions. Registration through the Madrid system does not create an 'international' registration, as in the case of the European CTM system, rather it creates a bundle of national rights, able to be administered centrally. Madrid provides a mechanism for obtaining trademark protection in many countries around the world, which is more effective than seeking protection separately in each individual country or jurisdiction of interest. As at 8 December 2008 there were 84 members comprising the Madrid Union of jurisdictions which have become party to the Agreement or the Protocol or both.

Certain countries and states will require a franchisor to have registered their Trade Mark in the country in question before they can register their franchise. It is important to be aware that different Trade Mark registering bodies take different approaches as to what they will register and what they won't. The registration process also takes different amounts of time and have different costs. In the UK, one would expect that a Trade Mark will take approximately six months to register from date of application to registration so long as it is not contested. In the US this is more likely to take twelve months. As soon as international franchising is considered, it is important to start the process of Trade Marking and protecting other Intellectual Property in the relevant countries.

International Franchise Models

There are two main franchise models to consider when franchising internationally:

- Master Franchising
- Franchisor led

Master Franchising

A master franchise model is where the franchisor sells the right to a country, state or province and the master franchisee is responsible for developing the franchise in their area. The master franchisee is usually responsible for helping to tailor the existing franchise model so that it is appropriate for the local or country market conditions that it will operate in. The master franchisee will also be responsible for to recruiting, training and supporting local franchisees.

In a number of master franchise models, the master franchisee is permitted to operate franchises that they own alongside other franchises that are recruited. This has the advantage that the master franchisee fully understands the franchised business as they are operating franchises themselves. In other master franchise models, the master franchisee is not permitted to operate any franchises themselves and must recruit external unit franchisees only. If a master franchisee is going to be permitted to operate their own franchises, it is important from a legal stance that they don't just operate franchises they own and don't recruit any external franchisees. Should a master franchisee only operate franchises that they own, their legal status will change from being a master franchisee to being an area or country developer. This may not be a problem however, it would mean a different Legal Agreement would need to be entered into.

The benefit of a master franchise model is that the franchisor will have someone who understands their local market and who is better placed to recruit, train and support franchisees than they can do from outside the country. The downside is that there is now another person in the franchisor/franchisee relationship that needs to make money.

Franchisor Led
The other way to franchise internationally is for the franchisor to undertake the role of tailoring the existing

franchise model to be suitable for each country they are going to franchise in. It is also the franchisor who will be responsible for recruiting, training and supporting the local franchisees. Realistically this can only be achieved by the franchisor having staff that are based in each locality often operating out of satellite offices. This has the advantage that the franchisors keep all the profit generated, however the franchisors costs will be increased. This model, whereby the franchisor manages the process themselves is not as stable a model as employees are more likely to move jobs than a master franchisee who has the franchise rights to a country or state for maybe twenty five years.

Whichever model one chooses to adopt for international franchising, it is critical that the person or people responsible for the local franchisees have a good knowledge and understanding of the market conditions and local traits and customs of the specific country.

Tailoring for International Markets

One of the biggest mistakes franchisors make when franchising internationally is that they try and replicate exactly the model that they have used domestically without considering the local customs, traits and market conditions in the countries they look to franchise in.

In the UK, a franchise territory may be based on a minimum number of people. This may be fine for the UK where population density is relatively high, however in a country such as Canada where the population density is much lower, operating the same territory criteria may prove to be logistically impractical and financial unviable. For a restaurant franchise in the UK the menu may need to be changed to take into account local tastes, customs and laws.

It is important that the franchisor undertakes prior research into local influencing factors

A restaurant franchise may make a significant amount of their profit from the sale of alcohol and this would have a big impact on the franchise model when operating in a country where the consumption of alcohol is prohibited. It is important that the franchisor undertakes prior research into these local influencing factors so that the Franchise Development model can be adapted to suit the country involved.

Every aspect of the Franchise Development Model used for the domestic franchise needs to be considered in light of each country one is looking to franchise within. This will include the cost of buying the franchise, the ongoing fee structure and how the franchise will be operated. Once a new Franchise Development model has been created that works for the country one is looking to franchise in, then all other elements involved in setting up a franchise, as described in Section 2 and Section 3 of this book need to be revisited and adjustments made accordingly. Once this has been done only then will the business be ready to start franchising internationally.

Local Expertise

It is virtually impossible to successfully franchise internationally without the advice and services of people that understand the local customs, traits and marketplace for each relevant country. It is also important to have advice from people who understand the local franchise market and laws in the relevant country. Although using local specialists will add to the cost of franchising internationally, without them it is likely that the franchise will fail in these countries resulting in a loss of time and money spent.

It is important to have advice from people who understand the local franchise market and laws in the relevant country

In many countries, national franchise associations have been created. These are a good starting point to find local specialists in franchising that can help international companies franchise successful in their country. A list containing information on many of the international franchise associations can be found on the

British Franchise Association's website at www.thebfa.org/international.asp.

If one is serious about franchising internationally a really good starting point is to visit some of the many franchise exhibitions and shows run in each country. Franchisors can see at first hand some of the competing franchises. It also enables them to speak to franchise professionals and attend seminars on franchising in the country.

However much one understands about franchising in ones own country, it is always advisable when franchising internationally to seek the advice and services of people that specialise in franchising in that country. Not only will this give a business the best chance of success in that country, but it will also ensure that they do not fall foul of any franchise or commercial legislation.

Franchising Internationally Summary

This chapter only touched on a few considerations for international franchising. It is therefore imperative to seek professional advice to ensure that a franchise can be adapted to meet the local customs, traits and market place that it is looking to operate within.

Franchising internationally can often cost more than when franchising in the UK. This is because it will involve both setting up of the franchise and the recruitment of master and local franchisees. However if done correctly, the rewards from international franchising, both financial and reputational are exceptional.

Chapter 16

FRANCHISE SALES

The final topic in this section relates to established franchise operations and is concerned with franchisee and franchisor sales. One of the key elements that differentiates a franchise from other forms of expansion is that the franchisee owns their business. If a franchisee owns a business, they have the right to sell it. Equally the franchisor will own their business and has the same right to sell their franchisor business should they so wish.

As with the last chapter on franchising internationally, there are many books written about how to sell franchisee and franchisor businesses. There are also companies that specialise in helping franchisees and franchisors to sell their businesses. Therefore I am only going to cover a couple of the key elements of franchise sales which are useful for companies considering franchising their business to be aware of.

Franchisee Sales

From a franchisor's perspective, it is important to understand that franchisees can and often do look to sell the franchises before the end of their initial or renewal franchise term. This may give rise to concern for businesses looking to franchise however it shouldn't.

There are many safeguards built into the Franchise Agreement to ensure that a sale can only take place to the right type of person

There are many safeguards built into the Franchise Agreement to ensure that a sale can only take place to the right type of person. Most franchise agreements will include a clause that gives the franchisor the first right to buy back the franchise. Where a franchisor does not wish to buy the franchise, the franchisor has the right to veto a sale to anyone that does not meet the criteria that would be required of a new franchisee.

Sometimes having new owners of a franchise can create a new drive and impetus to the business. This can help reinvigorate a franchise business that is meeting the minimum performance requirements, as stipulated in the Franchise Agreement, but not fully maximising the potential of their territory.

Although having a new person taking over franchisees can be a very good thing, there are some practical implications.

Firstly, the franchisor will have to vet any potential franchisee purchaser which will obviously take time for the franchisor. In order to compensate the franchisor for their time, it is usual that the franchisee is charged a sales application review fee. This fee is charged to the existing franchisee for each application the franchisor reviews regardless as to whether the sale goes through.

Secondly, the new person will need to be trained and will need a greater level of initial support than would be given to an established franchisee. In order to cover the cost of providing this training and extra ongoing support, it is usual for franchisors to charge the franchisee who sells their franchise a Transfer Fee. This Transfer Fee can either be a fixed amount or a percentage of the sales price.

Marketing a Franchisee Resale

If a franchisor decides not to take up the option to buy back the franchise, the franchisee will need to market their franchise for sale. Some franchisors will advertise franchise territories for sale on their website and will indicate which are new franchises and which are franchise resales. There are also a number of franchise website directories that list both new franchises and franchise resales as well as specialist franchise brokerage companies that have people on their book looking to buy franchise resales.

The franchise resale market is very active. This is because there are many people who like the concept of being a franchisee but also are attracted by the opportunity to buy into an existing business with an existing customer database. Given the benefits of buying an existing franchise business, franchise resales will command a higher value that a new franchise. Unfortunately there is no standard formula for calculating the value of a franchise resale. The price will be dependent on the profitability of the existing franchise, the additional potential within the territory, and what value other franchise resales are being priced at. What is worth stating is that the value of a franchise resale will normally be less than the value of a non franchised business being sold. This is because the franchised business being sold will have a limiting timescale that it can be operated for, whereas a non franchised business can potentially be run for ever.

Franchisee Resale Summary

Selling their franchise is a legal right for the franchisee. Therefore it is important that steps are taken to control and manage the way the franchise sale can happen when setting up the franchise at the outset.

Franchisor Sales

When setting up a franchised business it is important to know that should an opportunity arise or it becomes necessary to do so, a franchisor can sell their business. The franchisees within the network have no right or say over who buys the franchised business however the purchaser will take over the ownership and legal obligations for all the franchisees within the network.

Unlike the franchisee resale market, which is well publicised and opportunities can be seen in various media, franchisor sales are not surprisingly, less publicly known. If a franchisor is looking to sell, they may well not want their franchisee network to know about it due to the unsettling nature it may have. For this reason it is very unusual to see franchisor business being marketed openly. However this does not mean that there aren't franchisor businesses for sale. I spoke recently to a franchise sales company that specialises in both franchisee resales and franchisor sales and the managing director said that it is normal for them to have at least six franchisors looking to sell their business on their books at ay one time.

There are also companies that look to buy existing franchisor businesses and will approach franchisors directly. Companies do this for a number of reasons, some of which can include:

- It can provide the company with an opportunity to buy a business with an established network of franchisees through which they can they sell other complementary products and services.
- It can allow a foreign company with a quick way to enter the UK market.

- A company can operate the franchised business alongside an existing business, enabling it to share resources which in turn will cut the operating costs for both parts of the business.

It is also not uncommon for a franchisee or a group of franchisees within the network to buy the business from the franchisor. This has the advantage that the franchisee or franchisees understand the business well, and will provide a level of continuity to the franchise.

As with the value of franchisee resales, there is no standard formula for calculating the price of franchisor sales. The price that a franchisor business can command will vary dependent on the profitability of the business, the length of time remaining on each franchise agreement, the remaining capacity to sell franchises, and the market place that the franchised business operates within. As with anything one sells, it is more likely to get a better price if someone wants to buy it and approaches the seller, rather than the seller trying to convince someone to buy it.

It is important to consider the implications of selling the business in the future

When starting out on the process of franchising a business, it is important to consider the implications of selling the business in the future. Often companies will set up a separate franchise business with its own legal entity so that everything to do with the franchise is kept in one place. This is especially helpful if there are parts of the business that are not being franchised. Consideration should also be given as to who owns the intellectual property rights and whether this should be an individual owner of the business, the parent business or the franchised business.

Franchisor Sales Summary

Be aware that there is a market for franchisor sales, although not in the public domain, so unless approached directly by someone who wants to buy your business, it is likely that the services of a specialist franchise sales company will be required. And finally it is important to structure the franchised business correctly at the start of your franchise journey as it will make the job of selling the franchise a lot easier should the need arise.

SECTION 5

Useful Information

The information in this final chapter will provide an insight into franchise industry information and where to obtain further information and advice. In addition, other business expansion models will be explored for when franchising is not appropriate.

The final five chapters will cover the following areas:

Chapter 17 - History of Franchising
This chapter will cover the history of franchising, how and where it all started, how the franchise industry established itself in the UK and the current size of the UK franchise market.

Chapter 18 - Types of Franchises
This chapter looks at the differences between seven different types of franchises and the key characteristics of each.

Chapter 19 - Franchise Glossary of Terms
In franchising, specific words and terminology are used. This chapter will provide definitions in a clear and concise fashion.

Chapter 20 - Other Expansion Models
For those businesses where Full Business Format franchising is not appropriate, this chapter will give a brief summary of some other business

expansion models which will include: Other types of Franchise Models; Company Expansion; Licensing; Agencies; Distributorships; and Agencies.

Chapter 21 - Sources of help

In this final chapter I provide a selection of places where further information and advice on franchising can be found.

Chapter 17

HISTORY OF FRANCHISING

The term franchising can be traced back as far as the middle ages and was used to describe the granting of rights, usually by the monarch, to another individual to develop and govern over an area of land which belonged to the state. The franchisee was normally free to develop the land however they wished.

In the early nineteenth century franchising was used to define the act of voting local members of parliament. This was a widely abused and corrupt system with Boroughs consisting of a tiny number of electors voting in Members of Parliament. These Boroughs became known as "rotten boroughs". The most notorious example of a rotten borough was "Old Sarum", which was a motley collection of fields rather than a community. Nonetheless, its seven voters returned two Members of Parliament. The Great Reform Act of 1830 saw an end to the 56 rotten boroughs, the redistribution of some seats to the new cities and a slight reduction in property qualifications on voting. A new uniform franchise was introduced in the boroughs giving the vote to those who paid more than £10 a year in rates or rent. The next major step on the way to achieving universal suffrage took place in 1867. The Second Reform extended the franchise further enabling over two and a half million men to vote. By the time of the Third Reform Act of 1884, which equalised voting restrictions between counties and boroughs, over 50% of the adult male population were able to express their opinions through the ballot box.

Franchising was also the term used by the beer industry where many brewers allowed certain pubs to obtain leaseholds and sell their beer. In the nineteenth century when legislation was passed to control the widespread abuse of alcohol by imposing rules on the condition of places where alcohol could be sold. This made it too costly for many individuals to own licenced premises and consequently the rich brewers were concerned about the effect on their industry of the loss of independent pub owners. They came up with the plan of undertaking the costly compliance with the new legislation themselves, then offering local pub owners the opportunity to become franchise owners, paying a lease on the property and working closely with the owners at a local and national level. This is what we refer to today as the "Tied System".

The first "modern" franchise in terms closely linked to the franchising we know today can be traced to the US and "The

Singer Sewing Machine Company". Isaac Merritt Singer invented the Singer Sewing machine in 1850. The Singer Sewing Machine Company in the US had developed a way of mass producing sewing machines enabling them to be sold at a price accessible to the masses. However as more people became owners of Singer Sewing Machines throughout the US, the Singer Sewing Machine Company found it increasingly difficult to provide a service and replacement parts service. Its solution was to establish a nationwide service & maintenance franchise.

In the 1900's General Motors followed The Singer Sewing Company's approach to the motor industry by establishing a nationwide network of "dealers" who were granted the exclusive right to sell and service General Motor vehicles in specific areas of the country.

Throughout the middle half of the twentieth century more companies viewed franchising as a way of establishing both national and international coverage. The Wimpy brand was created by Eddie Gold of Chicago in the 1930s. The name was inspired by the character of J. Wellington Wimpy from the Popeye cartoons created by Elzie Crisler Segar. Eddie Gold was running 12 restaurants by the early 1950s, when the concept of fast food came to the attention of the directors of J. Lyons and Co. Lyons, they licensed the brand for use in the United Kingdom and in 1954 the first "Wimpy Bar" Lyons was established at the Lyons Corner House in Coventry Street, London. Originally the bar was a special fast-food section within the more traditional Corner House restaurants, but the success soon led to the establishment of separate Wimpy restaurants serving only hamburger based meals. By the early 1970s the business had expanded to over a thousand restaurants in 23 countries.

The franchising boom of the 1950s created the system, commonly known as the "Full Business Format Franchise". This acknowledged the franchise system as a distinct method of doing business rather than just having the rights to sell a product or services. The franchisee was buying a complete business package and the franchisor benefited from rapid growth with fewer resources than if they expanded through purely company owned outlets.

The popularity of franchising was affected in the 1960's as a direct result of events in both the UK and the US, which included the stock market turmoil in the US, and the fraudulent marketing scheme called pyramid selling in the UK.

The late 1970s saw the formation of the British Franchise Association (bfa) with the objective of stopping the corrupt franchise business practices in the UK. Within a short time the bfa earned all-party support in Parliament and its existence helped a period of rapid expansion of franchising in the UK. The founder members of the bfa include Dyno-Rod, Holiday Inns, Kentucky Fried Chicken, Prontaprint, ServiceMaster and Wimpy.

The size and reputation of the founders of the bfa brought about a level of credibility and respectability for both the bfa and franchising in the UK as a whole, This has led to the franchising sector being a major contributor to the UK economy. In 2009 the franchising sector was valued at £11.8 billion. The bfa went on to encourage banks to support franchising, and National Westminster, Barclays, Midland, Lloyds TSB and the Royal Bank of Scotland took the initiative and formed franchise departments.

In 2009 the franchise industry had, according to the bfa and NatWest annual franchise survey, 842 franchise brands. This figure for the number of franchised businesses in the UK has been open to dispute as a number of published franchise directories show the figure as being between 1,200 and 1,400. A copy of the bfa NatWest annual franchise survey can be purchase from the bfa's bookshop at www.thebfa.org.

Chapter 18

TYPES OF FRANCHISES

There are a large number of different types of franchises in the UK, the main ones being:

- Investment franchise
- Executive franchise
- Retail franchise
- Distribution franchise
- Depot franchise
- Job franchise
- Management franchise

Investment Franchise

In an investment franchise, the franchisee will buy the franchise but will not directly work in the business. Instead they employ their own management team and staff. Investment franchises are operated by the fast-food and restaurant chains, as well as by some well-known hotels.

Executive Franchise

An executive franchise involves the provision of professional services, such as financial advice, legal services or recruitment assistance. Executive franchises can be either single operator businesses or can involve the franchisee employing staff.

Retail Franchise

With a retail franchise, the franchisee will operate from premises selling products or services usually to walk in customers. Often, retail franchises will have to operate set opening times in keeping with other local stores. The franchisee is likely to have to employ staff to help run the business. One major factor in running a retail franchise is that it requires lots of customer interaction, and therefore excellent customer service is a high priority.

Distribution Franchise

A distribution franchise permits the franchisee to operate from a depot or central office that is owned by the franchisor. The franchisee will be responsible for delivering products either themselves or by employing additional staff.

Depot Franchise

In a depot franchise, the franchisee is the operator and sole occupant of the depot. This type of franchise is generally available to courier companies and parts suppliers, for whom a depot is an essential part of the business.

Job Franchise

A job franchise is usually a one-person business, operated by the franchisee either from home or a small office. Unlike many other types of franchises, job franchises can lend themselves to being operated as either a full time or part time business.

Management Franchise

A management franchise is where the franchisee will be responsible for both running the franchise and employing and managing a team of operatives. Management franchises tend to include office based work, and will include working closely with businesses and organisations to provide either a service or product. This type of franchise is often best for those with management experience and the ability to work with a number of staff.

Chapter 19

FRANCHISE GLOSSARY OF TERMS

BFA

The British Franchise Association was established in 1978 with the aim of regulating franchising on an ethical basis, by granting membership to those franchisors that it considers, meets the demands of its Codes of Ethics and procedures.

Business Format

The term used to describe a franchise where the franchisee buys into the total system of the brand, including the brand name, know-how, training, methodology, systems, procedures and ongoing product development.

Buy Back

Where the franchisor agrees to purchase the franchise back from the franchisee where the franchisee no longer wishes to continue.

Disclosure

The practice of revealing detailed information about the franchisor's business and franchise package, prior to the signing of the Franchise Agreement. This is a legal obligation in many European and North American countries, BUT only voluntary in the UK.

Exclusive Territory	The area within which a franchisee will operate and where they are the only person within the franchisee network that is permitted to proactively market their products or services.
Franchise Licence	The right to operate a franchise using the franchisor's brand name system of the brand, know-how, methodology, systems, and procedures for which an initial Licence fee is charged as well as Ongoing Fees.
Franchise Contract	Often referred to as the Franchise Agreement, and sets out the terms under which the Franchise Licence is granted.
Franchise	The business format being offered for sale under a Franchise Licence.
Franchisee	The person or company buying the Franchise.
Franchise Operations Manual	The detailed document or manual which describes every aspect of how the franchisee should run their franchise business.
Franchise Package	The goods and services that the franchisor will provide a franchisee, enabling them to launch their franchise business.
Franchisor	The company selling the original Franchise and providing the support to their franchisees.
Franchisor Management Fee	Sometimes referred to as a "Royalty" or "Ongoing Fees". These are the fees that the franchisee will pay the franchisor, usually monthly, as a fixed amount or a percentage of the franchisee's turnover.
Intellectual Rights	The franchisor's "secrets" of doing business including the various Trade Marks, Patents,

Branding, Manuals etc.

Master Franchise

A licence granted to an individual or company to operate in more than one territory; often Master franchises are granted for a whole Country or large Region.

P&L Projections

The calculations, based on the franchisor's experience, which predicts the franchisee's financial performance.

Pilot Operation

A test undertaken by the franchisor to assess how their franchise will operate and how successful it will be. The pilot is set-up in a separate geographic location and is run at arms distance from the franchisor to replicate how an independent franchisee should operate and perform.

Renewal

The legal provision for granting a further franchise term once the initial term has expired. Usually there are a range of conditions attached to any franchise renewal.

Re-sale

Refers to the sale of a franchise, by a franchisee, to another person or company other than the franchisor.

Royalties

Sometimes referred to as "Franchisor Management Fees" or "Ongoing Fees". These are the fees that the franchisee will pay the franchisor, usually monthly, as either a fixed amount or a percentage of the franchisee's turnover.

Term

Refers to the length of time the franchise is granted for.

Termination

The legal provision by which either party may terminate the Franchise Agreement, often used when the franchisee materially breaches the terms of the Franchise Agreement.

Trading Act

Known as the Trading Schemes Act (1996). This was introduced to combat the maligned practice of "pyramid selling".

Vertical Block Exemption

On 1st June 2010, revised European regulation came into force effecting Vertical Agreements, which are agreements entered into by parties at different levels of the supply chain, and which includes franchising. The Vertical Block Exemption exempts franchise agreements amongst others, from being restrictive agreements under Article 101 (ex Article 81) of the EU Treaty, so long as certain conditions are met.

Chapter 20

OTHER EXPANSION MODELS

This book has concentrated on the franchising model referred to as "Full Business Format Franchising". However, before starting out on this expansion route it is important to check whether this is the most appropriate way to expand the business. This chapter will explain the key characteristics of a number of other expansion models that business owners should consider before making their final decision as to the most appropriate way forward.

Other Franchise Models

Most people have heard the term franchising used in the media in connection with many things, from trains and cars, to sports teams, to being eligible to vote, and to celebrity product endorsements and Hollywood films. So, what are some of these other business models that use the term franchising?

In the case of the rail franchises, companies are granted the rights to operate train services for specific parts of the country. In order to keep the franchise they must meet certain targets such as number of services operated each day, train performance levels, however the company will operate under their own brand and run following their own operating guidelines.

In the world of sports, the term franchising is often used. Since its inception in 1926 the American Football League has referred to its teams as franchises. In these terms, franchising is used to mean the ownership of the League in which teams compete.

Franchising has over time been used to describe many different circumstances whereby individuals are granted certain rights

When a celebrity endorses and lends their name to a product or range of products such as Michael Jordan's AIR JORDAN shoe range, this is also referred to as franchising. Franchising in these terms relates the celebrities granting a right for a manufacturer to use their name in association with their products.

In the world of the movies, the term franchising is often used to describe a film that becomes part of a series and has associated merchandise. Star Wars and James Bond are both well known franchises with branded merchandise and associated activities all operating off the back of the success of the films.

Therefore franchising as a term, has over time, been used to describe many different circumstances whereby individuals are granted certain rights.

Company Expansion

It's easy when one starts thinking about franchising a business to forget that the most common way of expanding a business is through company owned expansion. It is important to take the time to asses whether expanding the business through company owned expansion is a viable option, as there are many benefits to expanding a business this way. As soon as a business expands using third parties, whether through franchising or any other expansion models, there will inevitably be some loss of control.

The most common way of expanding a business is through company owned expansion

There are a number of key considerations when deciding whether to expand a business through company expansion, which are:

Does the business have access to the funding required to open up new offices or outlets around the country?

The level of funding required will be different for every business and will depend on a number of factors such as: the need to set-up retail shops or commercial offices; the need number of staff required in each outlet; the number of outlets that are required and over what timescale.

Access to the necessary funding is a major consideration when undertaking company expansion. If the funds are not available, or cannot be raised, company expansion may not be right for the business.

Does the business want the issues and responsibilities that come with employing and managing large numbers of staff?

When expanding a business through company expansion, it is very likely that there will be a need to employ large numbers of staff. An existing business owner will know that employing staff comes with many legal and operational obligations. When growing through company expansion, businesses need to be prepared to take on these obligations. I am not trying to dissuade anyone from expanding through company expansion as this is how the majority of companies expand in the UK, however if a business wants to avoid the obligations that come when employing large number of staff then company expansion may not be right for the business.

Can you expand quickly enough through company expansion?

Often company expansion can be a slow process, unless the business has access to large funding streams. Most businesses that expand using company expansion do so by waiting until they have generated sufficient profits to either finance their second outlet from these profits or use the profits to secure bank or other forms of funding. Once the funding is in place the business will need to find a suitable location for the outlet, recruit and train the necessary staff and then start operating. Businesses usually then have to wait until the second outlet is generating sufficient profits to help finance a third outlet, and so the process goes on. This can be a slow process. If the speed of expansion is important then company expansion may not be right for the business.

Are you happy being liable for the actions of your staff?

An important consideration when using company expansion to grow a business is ensuring that the systems and processes can be put in place to ensure that the staff, based in other outlets, operate exactly as they should. It is important to remember that a business is liable for the actions of their staff.

If there are major concerns about how staff can be effectively managed or being liable for their actions, then company expansion may not be right for the business.

Licensing

Licensing as a form of business expansion is less well understood than company expansion or franchising. This is because licensing can take many forms. The simplest way of thinking about licensing is that the business (the licensor) grants someone (the licensee) the right to sell their products or services but under the licensees own company name. A licence is just a commercial contract laying out the terms that are agreed between two parties, and these terms can be whatever they like.

> *A licence is just a commercial contract laying out the terms that are agreed between two parties*

Without wishing to confuse anyone, it is worth stating that "Full Business Format Franchising" is a form of licensing, as the franchisor grants the franchisee some rights. However with a "Full Business Format Franchise", there are usually many more rights and obligations.

When deciding whether licensing is the right expansion model, one should consider the following questions:

What type of person is best to sell your products and services?

In most standard licence agreements, the licensee usually is an existing business owner with their own customer base. This means the licensor will not have to support their licensees as much as they would if they were staff or franchisees, as the licensee already understands how to run a business. The licensor's role is more focussed around the technical support relating to the product or service that is licensed and monitoring the way the licensees sell the licensed products or services. As the licensee trades under their own name, rather than that of the licensor, there is much less risk to the licensor's brand reputation. If a licensee causes problems then it is far easier to terminate their licence than compared to terminating a franchise. The downside is that the licensor's brand name does not get promoted. This is where a business must decide whether having individuals and companies trading under their brand name are important. If it is important to having people trading under the company's brand name then licensing may not be right for the business.

Is speed to market important?

As licensees are usually existing business owners, this means that they will already have their own customer database that they can market the licensed products or services to. As a result licensing allows businesses to get their products and services into the market place far quicker than they could if they had to set-up new outlets themselves. Setting up and getting any new outlet established, whether it is company owned or a franchise will inevitably take time.

It is also usual that licensees are granted on a non exclusive basis as the licensee isn't reliant on the income generated from selling just the licensed services or products since they still have the income from their own products and services. Licensees usually have no issue with non exclusive territories as they already have their own database of customers to sell to. This means that businesses have the potential to sell far more licenses than they could if they franchised. If speed of expansion or the number of outlets selling your products or services is important then licensing may be right for the business.

Do you want to be liable for the products and services sold?

As previously stated, the issue of liability is usually a major concern for businesses considering expansion. Businesses worry about how they will control the way their products or services are sold nationwide, particularly when they have a lot of people selling them. As with franchising, licensing removes most of the liability issues. With licensing, the legal contract for the sale of any product or service is between the customer and the licensee. The only time that a licensor could be liable is if they inform a licensee how to do something and the information they give is illegal. So if reducing the issue of liability is important then either licensing or franchising may be the right for the business.

Agencies

Often when people hear the words "Agents" or "Agency" they tend to think of door to door salespeople or Travel Agents. The key characteristic of an agency model is that the business takes on individuals or company's "Agents" to sell their products and services on their behalf. The door to door salesperson will sell products and services on behalf of the company they are representing. This is the same with Travel Agents who sell holidays on behalf of holiday companies. In both cases the customer is not signing with the Agent but with the original company. Therefore the company is liable for the actions of their Agents.

The company is liable for the actions of their Agents

In the case of Travel Agents most people do not have worry about buying their holiday through Travel Agents as they are very well regulated. The systems and processes adopted by the Travel Agents are very sophisticated and make it very difficult for them to miss sell. This is not always the case when it comes to other Agents such as the ones that knock on doors as in these cases it is likely that the Agent is on a sales commission and therefore can give rise to a "sell at any cost" approach. This is why there are instances of door to door sales agents staying in a house for many hours trying to convince the customer to buy, and not surprisingly this can lead to opportunities for miss selling.

When considering whether to adopt an Agency Model for expanding your business, these are some of the questions that should be asked:

Is speed to market important?

There are established lists of people who are prepared to act as Agents on behalf of companies. Therefore it can be relatively easy and quick to establish a network of Agents covering the whole country. In this respect Agency models allow quicker expansion than company owned expansion or franchising. If speed of expansion is important then an Agency model may be right for the business.

Do you want to be liable for the products and services sold?

The liability issue is the biggest concern that people have when considering expanding using an Agency model. It is important to consider whether systems and processes can be established which make it very difficult for miss selling by Agents. If systems and processes can be established then using Agents can be a quick route to market however if not, take care. If it is important to limit liability, then an Agency model may not be right for the business.

Do you want to avoid employing large numbers of staff?

Employing large numbers of staff and all that it entails is often the reason businesses look for other expansion models rather than company expansion. On the face of it, using Agents rather than staff may seem a good way to avoid staff issues. On one level that is correct as Agents are not employees and Agents do not have the same rights as an employee. However, under UK and European law, self-employed Agents are legally entitled to either indemnity or compensation arrangements should a business terminate their agreement with the Agent. With an indemnity agreement, the business has to pay an amount reflecting the value of the work the agent has done in building up the sales for the business, such as the Agent's efforts to identify customers and build relationships. With a compensation agreement, the business has to pay an amount reflecting the value of what the Agent has achieved, and the Agent's loss of future earnings such as the potential future sales to customers who the agent introduced. Therefore once a business has taken on Agents they cannot suddenly decide to terminate their contact with them without paying some form of compensation for their loss of earnings, unless of course the Agent was guilty of gross misconduct or a similar misdemeanour. In addition, if the Agent is self-employed, the business will be required to pay an indemnity or compensation if the agent dies or retires. Unless one is prepared to accept these conditions then an Agency model may not be right for the business.

Distributorships

Expansion using Distributors is mainly for businesses that have products. The business sells their products direct to a Distributor and the Distributor is responsible for selling products to their own customers. For many businesses, this has the attraction that once the product has been sold, they are no longer responsible.

The Distributor is responsible for selling products to their own customers

The key questions when considering whether to adopt a Distributorship model are:

Is brand development important?

Distributors sell the products under their own company name and therefore the brand of the originating company will have limited or no visibility to the customer. Typically the originating company's brand will only be seen on the product packaging. This is where one needs to differentiate between the brand name of the company and the brand name of the product. If awareness and promotion of the corporate brand is important then a Distributorship model may not be right for the business.

Is speed to market important?

Using a Distributor model is probably the quickest way to get products sold nationwide. There are no issues relating to commercial premises or staff as the Distributor buys the products and takes control of how to sell them. The down side is that the business has lost control over how products are sold or and displayed. The majority of Distributors also sell many competing products and therefore the business has very little control over the quantity and speed of products sold. If it is important how products are displayed, marketed and sold to customers then a Distributorship model may not be right for the business.

Do you want to be liable for the products and services sold?

As the business sells products to the Distributor, the responsibility and liability for these products theoretically ends for the business and then becomes the Distributor's concern. However, if the product is faulty then the business may still be liable. If the issue of liability is a major concern then a Distributorship model may be right for the business.

Acquisitions

Although not usually uppermost in most people's minds when considering expansion models for a business, Acquisitions should not be overlooked. Buying an established business and rebranding it can be a fast way of establishing and growing a brand. What may be surprising to learn is that it can be relatively easy to borrow the money to buy an established business, so long as it's not overpriced. Banks are prepared to lend against the trading history and profitability of existing businesses. When buying an existing business one usually buys the assets of the business, which will include items such as the fixtures and fittings. It is important to know however that under the Transfer of Undertakings (Protection of Employment) Regulations (TUPE)

When considering expansion Acquisitions should not be overlooked

it is very likely that the buyer will have to take on all the staff from the old business. This means that other than changing the name above the door, the business can carry on trading virtually immediately the purchase is completed. The downside is that the purchaser may have to take on unhappy or disillusioned staff. Consideration also needs to be given to the impact on the customers of the old company, as they may want to do business with the new owners.

When deciding whether expansion through acquisitions is the right model for your business these key questions should be asked:

Are there any suitable companies that you could buy?

If a business operates in a marketplace where there are many competitors, it is likely that some of these competitor companies may be open to acquisition; however it is important to only look to buy companies that are in the right location geographically and can easily work within the existing business. If there are competitor companies that operate in the areas where a business is looking to expand then expansion by acquisition may be right for the business.

Do you want to takeover staff from another company?

Given the Transfer of Undertakings (Protection of Employment) Regulations (TUPE) it is highly likely that any purchaser will have to take over the employment of the staff from the company being sold. This may mean that they will have no choice as to who they have as employees in the company they acquire. It could result in the purchaser inheriting some really good staff however equally they could be stuck with employees that they would rather not have. When considering an acquisition do not just think about the financial figures as the staff issues are equally important. If a business does not want to take on staff from another company then expansion by acquisition may not be right for the business.

Deciding which Expansion Model is Right

Every business is different and every business owner has different influencing factors. The decision as to which expansion model to adopt is likely to be one of the most important decisions a business takes, and therefore should not be rushed. It is important that total commitment is given to the model chosen otherwise there is a real risk of wasting a lot of money, effort and time. Worse still, the wrong decision could damage the business.

This may sound like a recommendation not to expand a business; however nothing could be further from the truth. I whole heartedly believe that done correctly expanding a business can be financially and morally fulfilling. The opportunity for a business owner to grow from a single outlet into a regional, national, and or international brand is challenging yet exciting and can provide business owners with an opportunity for far greater wealth and opportunities. Therefore it is essential to take time to objectively consider all the options then when a decision has been made, commit to it with total conviction and faith.

Chapter 21

SOURCES OF HELP

Listed below are a selection of organisations and sites that people considering franchising their business may find of help. Please note this is not an exhaustive list and there will be other places that there are other places where information can be found.

Selected Franchise Associations

- **The British Franchise Association**
  British Franchise Association, Centurion Court, 85f Milton Park, Abingdon, OX14 4RY
  Tel: 01235 820 470
  Email: mailroom@thebfa.org
  Web: www.thebfa.org

- **European Franchise Federation**
  179, ave. Louise, B-1050 Brussels, Belgium
  Tel: 00 32 2 520 16 07
  Email: info@eff-franchise.com
  Web: www.eff-franchise.com

- **International Franchise Association**
  1350 New York Avenue NW #900, Washington DC 20005, USA
  Tel: 001 202 628 8000
  Email: info@franchise.org
  Web: www.franchise.org

  For a full list of franchise associations visit:
  www.thebfa.org/international.asp

Banks with Dedicated Franchise Departments

- **Lloyds Banking Group**
  Franchise Unit, 2nd Floor, Northgate House, Kingsway, Cardiff, CF10 4LD
  Tel: 0800 587 2379
  Email: franchising@lloydstsb.co.uk
  Web: www.lloydstsb.com/franchising

- **NatWest**
  NatWest/RBS Franchise Team, 1st Floor, 280 Bishopsgate, London, EC2M 4RB
  Tel: 0800 092 917
  Email: franchise.retailbanking@natwest.com
  Web: www.natwest.com/business/services/market-expertise/franchising.ashx

- **The Royal Bank of Scotland plc**
  RBS Franchise Section, Level 1, 280 Bishopsgate, London, EC2M 4RB
  Tel: 0800 092 917
  Email: FranchiseRBS.RetailBanking@rbs.co.uk
  Web: www.rbs.co.uk/business/banking/g3/franchising.ashx

- **HSBC**
  Franchise Unit, 12 Calthorpe Road, Birmingham, B15 1QZ
  Tel: 0121 455 3438
  Email: franchiseunit@hsbc.com
  Web: www.hsbc.co.uk

Franchise Exhibition & Show Organisers

- **Venture Marketing Group**
  Tel: 020 8394 5226
  Email: adrian.goodsell@vmgl.com
  Web: www.franchiseinfo.co.uk

- **Prysm MFV**
  Tel: 0117 930 4927
  Email: simon@thefranchiseshow.co.uk
  Web: www.thefranchiseshow.co.uk

- **Job Done Marketing**
  Tel: 0116 242 4157
  Email: mark@jobdonemarketing.co.uk
  Web: www.jobdonemarketing.co.uk

Franchise Magazines

- **Business Franchise Magazine**
  6th & 7th Floor, 111 Upper Richmond Road, Putney, London, SW15 2TJ
  Tel: 020 8394 5216
  Email: alison@businessfranchise.com

- **Franchise World**
  Highlands House, 165 The Broadway, Wimbledon, London, SW19 1NE
  Tel: 020 8605 2555
  Email: info@franchiseworld.co.uk

- **The Franchise Magazine**
  Franchise House, 56 Surrey Street, Norwich, NR1 3FD
  Tel: 01603 620301
  Email: editorial@fdsltd.com

- **What Franchise Magazine**
  Partridge Publications, Third Floor, Gloucester House, Gloucester Mews, South Street,
  Eastbourne, East Sussex, BN21 4XH
  Tel: 01323 636004
  Email: richard@partridgeltd.co.uk

- **Making Money**
  Partridge Publications, Third Floor, Gloucester House, Gloucester Mews, South Street,
  Eastbourne, East Sussex, BN21 4XH
  Tel: 01323 636004
  Email: richard@partridgeltd.co.uk

Franchise Printed Directories

- **FranchiseWorld Directory**
  Tel: 020 8605 2555
  Email: nick@franchiseworld.co.uk
  Web: www.franchiseworld.com

- **The United Kingdom Franchise Directory**
  Tel: 01603 620301
  Email: richardc@fdsltd.com
  Web: www.theukfranchisedirectory.net

Newspapers that Cover Franchising

- **Daily Express**
  The Northern & Shell Building, 10 Lower Thames Street, London, EC3R 6EN
  Tel: 020 7098 2840
  Email: sean.hammond@express.co.uk

- **Daily Mail**
  5th Floor, Northcliffe House, 2 Derry Street, London, W8 5TT
  Tel: 0161 836 5001
  Web: www.mailclassified.co.uk

- **Daily Mirror**
  Tel: 020 7293 3434
  Email: simon.pitney@mgn.co.uk

- **Evening Standard**
  Northcliffe House, 2 Derry Street, London, W8 5EE
  Tel: 02073615008
  Email: sharon.webber@standatd.co.uk

- **Sunday Express**
  The Northern & Shell Building, 10 Lower Thames Street, London, EC3R 6EN
  Tel: 020 7098 2840
  Email: sean.hammond@express.co.uk

- **The Mail on Sunday**
  2 Derry St, London, W8 5TS Ms Joanne Beeney
  Tel: 0207 9387312
  Email: joanne.beeney@mailonsunday.co.uk

Franchise Website Directories

- **Business Franchise**
  Tel: 020 8394 5283
  Email: Nathalie@businessfranchise.com
  Web: www.businessfranchise.com

- **Franchise Direct**
  Tel: 03531 865 6370
  Email: brian@franchisedirect.co.uk
  Web: www.franchisedirect.co.uk

- **Franchise World**
  Tel: 020 8605
  Email: nick@franchiseworld.co.uk
  Web: www.franchiseworld.com

- **Making Money**
  Tel: 01323 636000
  Email: richard@partridgeltd.co.uk
  Web: www.makingmoney.com

- **Selectyourfranchise**
  Tel: 023 8027 5710
  Email: steve@selectyourfranchise.com
  Web: www.selctyourfranchise.com

- **What Franchise**
  Tel: 01323 636000
  Email: mark@partridgeltd.co.uk
  Web: www.whatfranchisemagazine.co.uk

- **Whichfranchise.com**
  Tel: 0141 204 0050
  Email: enquiry@whichfranchise.com
  Web: www.whichfranchise.com

Business
Options™

The Specialist
Franchise and Business Expansion
Consultancy

Business Options are one of the country's leading franchise and business expansion consultancies with over 20 years experience, both nationally and internationally within the franchising sector.

Our experienced consultants provide independent and plain speaking advice on all aspects of franchising a business and where franchising is not the most appropriate expansion model for a company, we can discuss other forms of business expansion too.

Business Options is the *only* consultancy accredited by:
British Franchise Association
Irish Franchise Association
Institute of Business Consultancy

Whatever your business,
we make it our business to make it a real success.

Contact Business Options for FREE advice on franchising or any other form of business expansion

info@businessoptions.biz   01420 550890   www.businessoptions.biz

INDEX